Simple Ingredients

Straightforward Recipes

Mouthwatering Meals

One Pound Meals

PHOTOGRAPHY
DAN JONES

DESIGN
SUPERFANTASTIC

MIGUEL BARCLAY'S

ONE POUND MEALS

FAST &
FRESH

www.onepoundmeals.com

CONTENTS

In true One Pound Meals style, this book has a laid back approach with no chapters. So just get stuck in, flick through my recipes and see what grabs your attention. I have listed every recipe here and thrown in a few helpful hashtags too.

#VEGETARIAN

#FISHANDSEAFOOD

Fish en Papillote 78

Fisherman's Pie 160

Hot Salad Niçoise 152

Mackerel Fish Cakes & Parsley Sauce 100

Neptune Pizzetti 146

Pad Thai 158

Pesce Al Forno 202

Sardine Pasta 116

Seafood Bisque 48

Singapore Chow Mein 70

Smoked Mackerel Paté 36

Smoky Fish Tacos 136

Tom Yum Soup 34

White Bean Fish Cassoulet 40

#CHICKEN

Cajun Chicken with Creamed Corn 142

Chicken & Chickpea Stew 196

Chicken & Mushroom Orzo 164

Chicken & Mushroom with Tobacco Fries 58

Chicken & Tenderstem Stir-fry 106

Chicken Noodle Soup 192

Chicken with Black Bean Sauce 82

Churrasco Burger 184

Pot Noodle 200

Spring Chicken 38

£1 Sticky Wings 110

Summer Chicken Pie 130

#MEAT

Bacon & Asparagus Tagliatelle 66

Bacon & Kale Minestrone Soup 86

Broad Bean Summer Cassoulet 126

Butternut Gnocchi with Crispy Parma Ham & Feta 128

Chicharos 194

Chilli Beef Ramen 104

Chorizo & Red Pepper Orzotto 180

Chorizo-Stuffed Sweet Potato 188

Goats' Cheese 'Scallops' 32

Griddled Peach, Parma Ham & Stilton Salad 28

Halloumi Kebab 144

Hasselback Squash 26

Keema Rice Pot 186

Lamb Meatball Tagine 76

Lamb Samosas 172

Mujadarra Wrap 74

Party Pizzas 118

Pork Char Sui 140

Pork Saltimbocca & Green Pea Mash 138

Pork Stir-Fry with Sugar Snap Peas 132

Sausage & Kale Omelette 182

Sausage, Kale & Black Bean Stew 92

Spanish Chorizo Stew 30

Speedy Chorizo Bolognese 134

Sticky Chilli Beef Bao 190

Ultimate £1 Rosti 162

GOING
FAST & FRESH

WOW! The response to my first book, *One Pound Meals*, really took me by surprise, so a big thank you to everyone who has helped make my ultra-simple and budget-friendly style of cooking a real alternative to some of the overcomplicated cookbooks out there.

It was so much fun to see *One Pound Meals* in the book charts alongside some of the biggest chefs in the world. Who could have imagined that? Some guy in his kitchen in Camden, cooking to a £1 budget, making paella with long-grain rice and a chicken stock cube, taking photos on his phone and uploading them to Instagram. It's definitely not the conventional way to do it.

So, here's my second book. I'm still working to a £1 budget, but I've moved with the seasons and this is a book for the warmer months. I've gone FAST & FRESH with my One Pound Meals: my focus is on making you feel good with delicious, quick and simple dishes that are light and vibrant, hitting that £1 budget without compromising on flavour.

Enjoy,

Miguel

WHAT'S NEW?

The feedback you gave me from *One Pound Meals* was that you guys loved the speed and simplicity of my recipes, so I've turned this up a notch for you and have created even more super-fast recipes for this book. I've also devised more of my characteristic One Pound Meals shortcuts to get you cooking fun and exciting dishes every day of the week without spending hours in the kitchen.

I was inspired by all the amazing food from around the globe, especially the street food in Thailand and the refreshing noodle and rice dishes from China. And then, from Europe, I've gone once again to the Mediterranean, taking inspiration from their simple, rustic fish dishes that I love so much. These guys adore their food and live in glorious sunshine, so they know how to balance flavours to create light and uplifting summer dishes.

SEASONAL PRODUCE

Choose seasonal foods, because they are way cheaper. For me, the most exciting food season in the UK is definitely when asparagus arrives. It's a real celebration of British produce and because the shop shelves are stacked with bunches at low prices, it's a great chance to make all these amazingly fresh asparagus dishes without blowing the budget. However, as soon as the season is over, prices rocket as they are flown in from around the globe (and quality plummets), so this is when you have to get clever by substituting asparagus with other vegetables such as Tenderstem broccoli, green beans or even roasted carrots, to bring the dish back under £1.

FROZEN FOOD

To create fast and fresh food with a more summery vibe, I found myself leaning more on frozen food, particularly frozen veg. Picked at their peak and then quickly frozen, the peas and broad beans I use in this book are really fresh and vibrant, and create zero waste because you only use what you need and the rest keeps for months in the freezer. This is key to saving money. It doesn't matter if an ingredient is fantastic value; if you throw away half the packet, then it has actually cost you double.

My other top tip is to cook with frozen fish. This is a game-changer for anyone who wants to eat healthier food on a budget – frozen fillets are amazing value, really easy to cook and so versatile. With one packet of fillets, I have created some vastly different fish dishes for this book.

MY
ONE POUND MEALS
APPROACH

You'll recognise my signature One Pound Meals style by how easily these recipes will fit in with your daily life. It's Tuesday, you've had a hard day at work, you peek into your fridge, then 20 minutes later you're sitting down to a fun and exciting plate of food.

That's the point of One Pound Meals, and this is how I created my Fast & Fresh collection:

FAST

By cooking on such a tight budget, you only need the core ingredients that provide the essential flavours to a dish, and this eliminates so many steps in both preparation and cooking. One Pound Meals are quicker, easier and create less mess than typical cookbook recipes. But, for this book, I wanted to take this one step further and create hassle-free recipes that contained only one or two simple steps, with loads of shortcuts, to create delicious meals with bold flavours that you can cook every day of the week.

FRESH

Focusing on using more fresh produce means dishes with brighter colours, packed with vegetables, full of zingy flavours and with faster cooking times. This fresh style of cooking maximises the taste of these ingredients, creating vivid summery dishes that celebrate healthy eating. By cooking from scratch with fresh ingredients you can control exactly what you eat, giving processed food and preservatives a miss.

DELICIOUS

My aim is to motivate you to cook as many recipes as possible by making them as irresistible as I can. I want you to keep cooking from my books, discovering one recipe after another, using up ingredients as you go along.

SIMPLE

My simple steps to amazing meals will give you the confidence to get into the kitchen and start creating fun and interesting food. With One Pound Meals it's easy to create dishes you've never eaten before, and by using familiar techniques, I've ensured you'll still be well inside your comfort zone while making dishes as exotic as Tom Yum Soup.

FAMILIAR

As with my first book, *One Pound Meals*, I have focused on my usual group of core ingredients that you'll find in most supermarkets, so you can switch from one book to the other when you have leftover ingredients to use up. The core ingredients are normal everyday staples that form the building blocks of many dishes, like onions, carrots and chicken. These are ingredients you will already be familiar with and comfortable with preparing, and you'll probably already have them in your fridge. So, I hope that if you are new to One Pound Meals, jumping into the mind-set is only a minor adjustment to your normal everyday routine.

ALL RECIPES
ARE FOR A SINGLE
SERVING

Remember that all my recipes are for one person.

MORE THAN ONE PERSON?

Just multiply the ingredients – because they are so straightforward, it's no trouble at all to calculate.

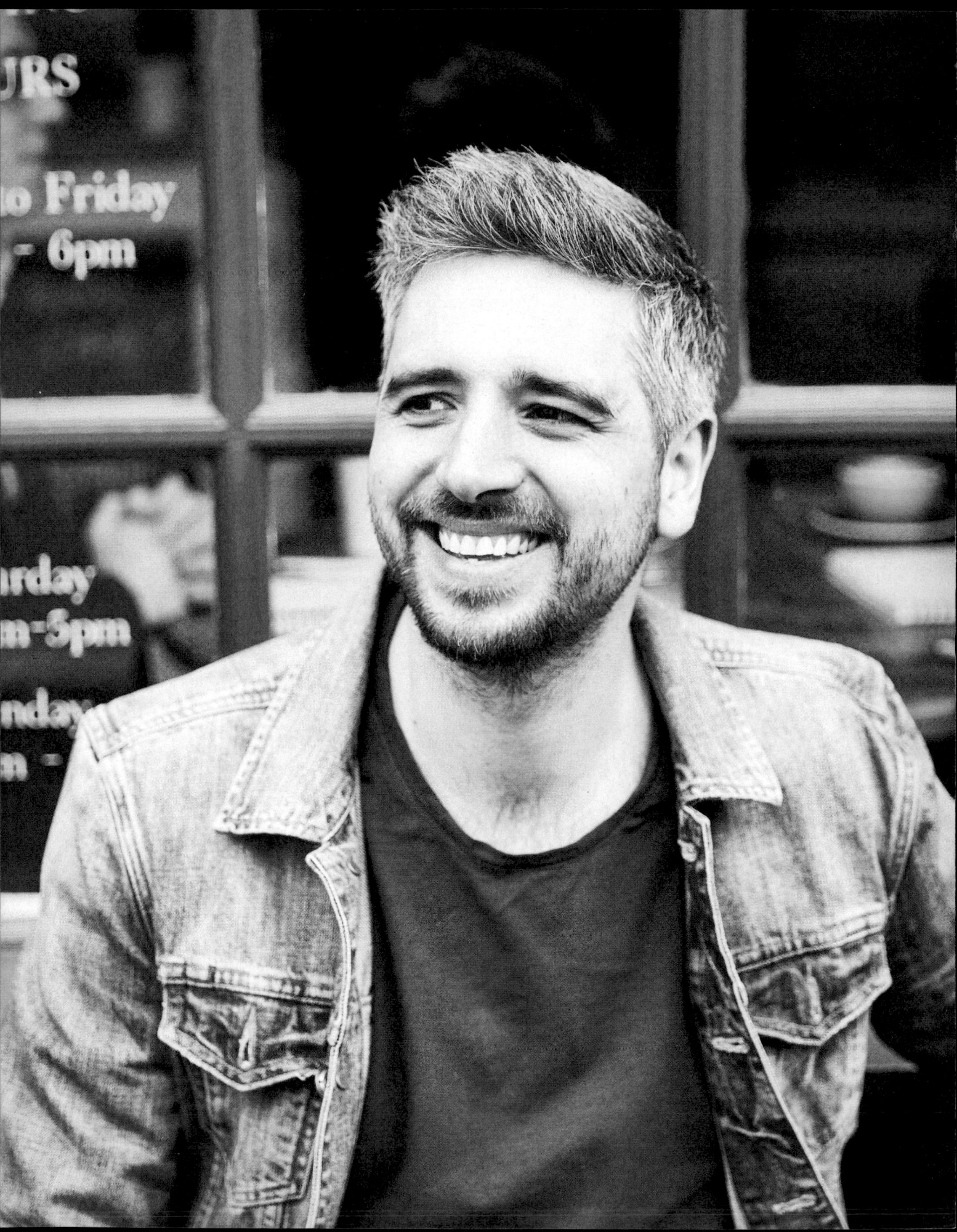
URS
to Friday
- 6pm
urday
m-5pm
nday

ALL FOR £1

This book is a step-by-step guide to slashing your food bills. I've done the hard work for you. So all you have to do is follow my lead to eat delicious, good-quality food every day.

Each recipe has been created to cost you less than £1 per portion (excluding salt, pepper and olive oil), and because I've designed them to use a core group of ingredients, you can plan your meals by using recipes with overlapping ingredients, helping you to get the most out of your shopping and eliminate waste from your kitchen bin.

Feel free to upgrade ingredients, though. This book is a blueprint to cooking cost-effective tasty meals, but if you want to use organic vegetables and fruit, you'll still make huge savings. The same goes for meat and herbs: swap chicken thigh for chicken breast or dried parsley for fresh. Whatever your preference, just do whatever makes you happiest (or use whatever you have left in the fridge!).

So, for those of you who are already living the One Pound Meals quick and easy lifestyle, this book will save you even more time and money. And for those of you who are new to this, welcome to the

ONE POUND MEALS REVOLUTION

YOGURT & HONEY POT

When I first moved to London, I used to get these on the way to work every day and eat them at my desk. But this was an expensive habit, so one day I had a go at making them myself and never looked back.

To make 1 portion

Handful of rolled oats

Handful of trail mix (just nuts and dried fruit)

3 tbsp honey

½ mug of Greek yogurt

To cook

Preheat your oven to 190°C/gas mark 5.

Combine the oats, trail mix and 1 tablespoon of the honey in a bowl then spread the mixture out evenly on a baking tray. Bake in the oven for 10 minutes until lightly toasted. Remove from the oven and leave to cool.

In a jar, add the rest of the honey, then the yogurt and top with your homemade crunchy granola.

GREEN SHAKSHUKA

This is my updated summer shakshuka recipe using fresh greens and a crumbling of salty feta cheese. A great idea for a fantastic, bright and healthy one-pan brunch.

To make 1 portion

A few spring onions, chopped

Handful of frozen peas

Handful of spinach

1 egg

20g feta cheese, crumbled

Olive oil

Salt and pepper

To cook

Pan-fry the spring onions in a splash of olive oil over a medium heat for a couple of minutes.

Meanwhile, defrost the peas in a colander under the hot tap.

Add the peas to the pan along with the spinach and a big pinch of salt and pepper and continue to fry for a minute.

Crack the egg on top of the peas, spinach and spring onions, then place a lid or plate on top of the pan. After about 3 minutes, when the egg white is cooked but the yolk is still runny, remove the pan from the heat, sprinkle over the crumbled feta and some cracked black pepper and serve straight from the pan.

PEA SOUP WITH PARMESAN 'CORAL'

My One Pound Meals pea soup is so quick and simple that I had to add a touch of flair with the parmesan 'coral' so that I could actually call it a proper recipe! This soup has a stunning vibrant green colour, and it tastes phenomenal.

To make 1 portion

Big handful of frozen peas

Small handful of grated parmesan

½ vegetable stock cube

Salt and pepper

To cook

Preheat your oven to 190°C/gas mark 5.

Bring a pan of salted water to the boil and cook the peas.

While the peas are cooking, pile the grated parmesan in a crisp-like shape on a non-stick baking tray and cook in the oven for about 5 minutes until melted but not browned. Gently peel the parmesan 'coral' off the tray and allow to cool and harden.

Drain the peas (keeping a mugful of the cooking water) and blitz them in a blender or food processor, along with about half the retained water and the stock cube until smooth. Season with salt and pepper and, depending on the consistency you want the soup to have, add more water to thin it.

Serve in a bowl with the parmesan 'coral' and a sprinkle of cracked black pepper to garnish.

GOAN CAULIFLOWER CURRY

You wouldn't expect it, but this dish actually has no cream in it. By using just flour and milk, you can create an amazingly rich and creamy sauce with a fraction of the calories, without compromising on eating the food you love.

To make 1 portion

¼ cauliflower

¼ white onion, sliced

1 tsp curry powder

1 tsp turmeric

1 tsp plain flour

200ml milk

Handful of spinach

Olive oil

Salt and pepper

To cook

Cut the cauliflower into individual florets and gently pan-fry them with the onion in a splash of olive oil over a medium heat. After about 5 minutes, add the curry powder, turmeric and flour, season well with salt and pepper then fry for a further minute until the onion is soft.

Slowly add the milk, stirring to create a sauce, then simmer gently for 15 minutes, stirring occasionally.

One minute before serving, add the spinach and stir it into the sauce, allowing it to wilt slightly.

Serve in a shallow bowl and enjoy.

HASSELBACK SQUASH

Hasselback potatoes are a fun and exciting way to cook potatoes if you are bored of the usual chips, wedges and mash. So, I took this style of preparation and made it into a main meal by creating a hasselback butternut squash. If you wanted to make this into a vegetarian recipe, then you can simply leave out the Parma ham.

To make 1 portion

½ butternut squash, seeds scraped out

2 slices of Parma ham, each halved

20g feta cheese, crumbled

1 tsp dried oregano

Olive oil

Salt and pepper

To cook

Preheat your oven to 190°C/gas mark 5.

Cut four v-shaped slits into the squash, making sure you don't cut all the way through.

Fold the pieces of Parma ham in half and lay one in each slit, then fill with a combination of crumbled feta and oregano, pressing it into the slits using your fingers.

Drizzle with olive oil, season with salt and pepper, then bake in the oven on a baking tray for about 30 minutes, until the squash is cooked all the way through.

GRIDDLED PEACH, PARMA HAM & STILTON SALAD

This classic combination of sweet and salty flavours creates an exciting, vibrant salad. Adding a warm ingredient also gives this dish an extra dimension and a bit of stimulation for the senses.

To make 1 portion

½ peach, cut into wedges

2 slices of Parma ham, each halved

Handful of rocket

Handful of crumbled stilton cheese

Olive oil

Salt and pepper

To cook

Heat a dry griddle pan or frying pan until hot (using a griddle pan will give the peach slices those lovely dark char marks), add the peach wedges and cook for a couple of minutes on each side until caramelised.

Arrange the griddled peach wedges on a plate with the Parma ham, rocket and crumbled stilton. Season with salt and loads of pepper, then drizzle over some olive oil.

SPANISH CHORIZO STEW

This is a quick and easy dish that uses the powerful flavours of chorizo to infuse these ordinary storecupboard ingredients and create an amazingly simple stew in just minutes. Frying the chorizo and releasing those paprika-infused oils at the start gives the dish a sturdy flavour base and means you can bypass the slow cooking that stews normally require.

To make 1 portion

Handful of cooking chorizo, sliced

½ white onion, sliced

200g chickpeas (from a 400g tin), drained

200g chopped tomatoes (from a 400g tin)

1 tsp paprika

Handful of spinach

Olive oil

Salt and pepper

To cook

Heat a glug of olive oil in a frying pan over a medium heat, then add the chorizo and fry for a few minutes until it starts to brown. Add the sliced onion and cook for a further minute until it starts to go translucent. Add the chickpeas and fry for a couple of minutes, coating everything in the paprika-infused oils, then add the chopped tomatoes and paprika, season with salt and pepper and simmer for 5 minutes until the sauce has thickened.

Just before serving, stir in the spinach until it wilts. Serve the stew with a drizzle of olive oil and plenty of cracked black pepper.

GOATS' CHEESE 'SCALLOPS'

I wanted to post this on Instagram so badly, but this dish was on the shortlist for the book cover, so I had to keep it under wraps for ages. They aren't really scallops – that would be way too expensive for One Pound Meals. Instead, I had a bit of fun by using goats' cheese presented in the style of scallops on a vibrant bed of bright green peas.

To make 1 portion

Handful of breadcrumbs (grated stale bread)

1 garlic clove, crushed

Goats' cheese, cut into 1cm-thick circles

1 rasher of smoked streaky bacon, roughly chopped

Handful of frozen peas

Olive oil

Salt and pepper

To cook

Preheat the grill to a medium heat.

Combine the breadcrumbs with a splash of olive oil, the crushed garlic, and some salt and pepper in a bowl. Lay the goats' cheese circles on a baking tray, then top them with the breadcrumbs and place under the grill for a couple of minutes until the breadcrumbs are nicely toasted and golden brown. Remove from the grill and set aside.

Then, pan-fry the bacon in a glug of olive oil over a medium heat.

Meanwhile, defrost the peas in a colander under the hot tap. Once the bacon starts to crisp, add the peas and continue to cook for 1–2 minutes. Pop the peas using the back of a spoon and season with salt and pepper.

Serve the peas and bacon in a shallow bowl and top with the goats' cheese 'scallops'.

TOM YUM SOUP

This was such a fun and daring dish to try to recreate. Using simple ingredients that you probably already have in your kitchen, in just 5 minutes you'll be tasting one of the most vibrant dishes in the world. This version of Tom Yum Soup, which is famous for its complex flavour combinations, is proof that eating on a budget can excite your taste buds and get you to re-evaluate the possibilities of what you can achieve in your kitchen at home.

To make 1 portion

Sesame oil

1 spring onion, roughly chopped

1 tsp hot paprika

½ chicken stock cube

300ml milk

Small handful of cooked and peeled prawns

¼ lemon

1 tbsp honey

Salt and pepper

To cook

Put a saucepan over a medium heat, add a splash of sesame oil and the chopped spring onion and fry for about 30 seconds, then add the paprika, crumble in the stock cube and stir in the milk.

Stir to combine everything, then add the prawns.

Simmer gently for 3 minutes, then squeeze in the juice from the lemon and stir in the honey.

Serve in a bowl and drizzle with sesame oil. It's as easy as that!

SMOKED MACKEREL PATÉ

This is something I make all the time. I love the smoky flavour of the mackerel and the way it balances so perfectly with the crème fraîche. This is a sophisticated tuna mayo for hipsters, so make sure you have char lines on your toasted sourdough bread!

To make I portion

1 smoked mackerel fillet, flaked

1 tbsp crème fraîche

2 slices of sourdough bread

Small handful of rocket

Olive oil

Salt and pepper

To prepare

Mix the mackerel and the crème fraîche together in a bowl, then season with a tiny bit of salt and loads of pepper.

Heat a dry griddle pan over a high heat. Drizzle both sides of the bread slices with olive oil, add a sprinkle of salt then griddle on each side, until toasted, with char marks.

To serve, spread the mackerel paté on the toast thickly and garnish with a few rocket leaves and more black pepper.

SPRING CHICKEN

This truly is spring on a plate! Gorgeous crispy-skinned chicken cooked really simply with just salt and pepper, on a bed of bright and vivid al dente spring vegetables in a chicken broth.

To make 1 portion

1 chicken thigh, de-boned

½ carrot, cut into strips

2 spring onions, roughly chopped

1 tsp plain flour

½ chicken stock cube

200ml water

Handful of frozen broad beans

Olive oil

Salt and pepper

To cook

Season the chicken thigh with salt and pepper and pan-fry it skin-side down in a splash of olive oil over a medium heat for 8 minutes until the skin is crispy. Turn the chicken over and cook for a further 8 minutes, until cooked through. Remove the chicken from the pan and set it aside.

Add the carrot and onions to the same pan and fry for a couple of minutes, then stir in the flour. Crumble in the stock cube and add the water, stirring continuously to ensure the stock cube dissolves. Season, simmer for a couple of minutes, then add the frozen broad beans and continue to simmer for a few minutes until the carrots are cooked but still firm.

Serve the vegetables and chicken broth in a bowl with the crispy-skinned thigh on top and cracked black pepper to garnish.

WHITE BEAN FISH CASSOULET

Frozen fish is a great no-hassle ingredient for cooking elegant and sophisticated meals on a budget. So if you haven't already tried using it, just grab yourself a bag and give this recipe a go. You won't believe that with just two minutes prep and an awkwardly balanced frozen fillet, you'll be sitting down to eat this amazing White Bean Fish Cassoulet.

To make 1 portion

¼ leek, rinsed and cut into roughly 7mm-thick circles

200g cannellini beans (from a 400g tin)

1 garlic clove, crushed

20ml milk

1 frozen white fish fillet

Olive oil

Salt and pepper

To cook

Preheat your oven to 190°C/gas mark 5.

Throw the leek circles into an ovenproof dish, along with the cannellini beans, garlic and milk.

Season well with salt and pepper, give it a quick stir and place the frozen fish fillet on top, straight from the freezer. Drizzle everything with a big glug of olive oil and don't forget to season the fish with salt and loads of cracked black pepper (the oil will help it stick to the fish).

Bake for about 25 minutes, until the fish is cooked through.

SPROUT & STILTON RISOTTO

Let's cook these sprouts in an inventive and creative way, and prove just how tasty they can be! They are a great vegetable with a lovely depth of flavour that can more than handle being the star ingredient alongside powerful stilton in this tasty risotto.

To make 1 portion

¼ onion, diced

Handful of Arborio risotto rice

½ vegetable stock cube

Kettle full of boiling water

Handful of sprouts, sliced

20g stilton cheese, crumbled

Olive oil

Salt and pepper

To cook

Pan-fry the onion in a splash of olive oil over a medium heat and add a pinch of salt and pepper. After 5 minutes, when the onion is slightly translucent in colour but before it starts to brown, throw in the rice and toast it for 1 minute with the onion.

Crumble in the stock cube and add about half a mug of boiling water from the kettle. Simmer and stir the rice continuously until most of the water is absorbed, then add more water. Repeat this process of adding water in small amounts as you continue to stir (you'll need about 500ml in total). After about 20 minutes of adding water and stirring the rice, give it a taste and, once you have that perfect firm but creamy texture, remove from the heat.

Meanwhile, pan-fry the sliced sprouts in a splash of olive oil over a medium-high heat with plenty of salt and pepper until the edges just start to go golden brown.

Add most of the stilton along with most of the fried sprouts to the risotto. Stir until the stilton melts, then serve the risotto in a bowl, garnishing it with the remaining crumbled stilton and sprouts, along with some cracked black pepper.

ROASTED VEGETABLE MILLEFEUILLE

Another great vegetable dish to impress your veggie mates with! Inspired by a famous French dessert, the vegetables are cooked in the oven and the dish is quickly assembled just before serving, to show off the lovely fresh veg to the fullest.

To make 1 portion

Handful of cherry tomatoes

A few asparagus spears

1 big sheet of filo pastry

A splash of milk .

10g feta cheese, crumbled

Olive oil

Salt and pepper

To cook

Preheat your oven to 190°C/gas mark 5.

Toss the tomatoes and asparagus in an ovenproof dish with a glug of olive oil and a generous pinch of salt and pepper and roast for 25 minutes.

Next, prepare the filo. You need 2 stacks of about 7 slim lengths of filo pastry cut to about 7 x 3cm. The easiest and neatest way to cut them is to fold the filo pastry sheet to create 7 layers and cut them all at once into two stacks with a sharp knife. Brush the top layer and the sides of each stack with milk, then lay each stack on a baking tray. Bake in the oven for about 15 minutes, or until the pastry is a lovely golden brown.

To assemble the millefeuille, simply arrange the tomatoes into two lines on a dish, balance one of the pastry stacks on top, then top with the asparagus. Add another pastry stack to the pile and finally top with crumbled feta and some cracked black pepper.

MEXICAN TORTILLA SOUP

This is a bold-flavoured, substantial and chunky soup that requires no blender. Just let it simmer away while you make some homemade tortilla chips to dip into it.

To make 1 portion

½ red onion, roughly diced

200g mixed beans (from a 400g tin), drained

100g sweetcorn (from a 400g tin), drained

200g chopped tomatoes (from a 400g tin)

1 tsp ground cumin

2 tsp smoked paprika

40g plain flour, plus extra for dusting

25ml water

Splash of single cream

Olive oil

Salt and pepper

To cook

Preheat your oven to 190°C/gas mark 5.

Fry the onion in a saucepan in a splash of olive oil over a medium heat for a few minutes until soft, then add the beans, sweetcorn, chopped tomatoes, cumin, 1 teaspoon of the paprika and plenty of salt and pepper. Stir, then simmer for about 15 minutes until the soup has thickened.

While the soup is cooking, mix the flour and water in a bowl with a pinch of salt and a pinch of paprika to form a dough. Dust the worktop with a little flour, then knead the dough on the worktop for a few minutes until smooth. Roll the dough out until it is about 20 x 20cm and lay it on a non-stick baking tray. Cut it into triangles (or any shape you want) and bake in the oven for about 10 minutes until crispy.

Serve the soup in a bowl with the cream and dust the tortilla chips with a pinch of salt and a pinch of paprika.

SEAFOOD BISQUE

This dish looks so posh! But, it's actually just some pan-fried cherry tomatoes with some frozen seafood. This is my sort of cooking: a few simple ingredients, very little effort and something restaurant-y in under 20 minutes.

To make 1 portion

¼ onion, roughly diced

A few cherry tomatoes, quartered

1 garlic clove, sliced

Pinch of dried chilli flakes

1 frozen white fish fillet

Small handful of cooked and peeled prawns

Pinch of dried (or chopped fresh) parsley

2 slices of bread

Olive oil

Salt and pepper

To cook

Pan-fry the onion and tomatoes in a glug of olive oil over a medium heat for a few minutes. Just before the onion starts to colour, add the garlic and chilli flakes.

Meanwhile, cut the frozen fish fillet into four pieces using a serrated knife and, just before the garlic starts to brown, add it to the pan along with a big splash of water. Simmer for about 15 minutes until the fish is cooked, adding the prawns after 10 minutes, then remove from the heat and garnish with the parsley.

For the bread, simply rub a little olive oil and salt into each side of the bread slices and either griddle them or toast them in a pan, until charred or browned on both sides.

PEA CANNELLONI

Frozen peas are such a versatile ingredient, and a great way of eating economically. With zero waste, they're ready at a moment's notice, straight from the freezer. But, instead of using them as a side dish, why not make them the star of the show with my take on an Italian classic – a fresh and vibrant Pea Cannelloni with a tangy feta cheese topping.

To make 1 portion

2 big handfuls of frozen peas

3 dried lasagne sheets

Small handful of crumbled feta cheese

Olive oil

Salt and pepper

To cook

Preheat your oven to 190°C/gas mark 5 and bring a pan of salted water to the boil.

Add the peas and the lasagne sheets to the boiling water and bring back to the boil. As soon as the water starts to boil (and the lasagne sheets are floppy), drain the peas, remove the part-cooked lasagne sheets and set them aside.

Put the peas in a bowl, pop them all with the back of a tablespoon to break their skins, then add a generous glug of olive oil and season with salt and pepper.

Place a few spoonfuls of peas on each lasagne sheet and roll them into tubes. Lay the filled tubes in a small ovenproof dish and scatter over the crumbled feta, adding a glug of olive oil and sprinkling over some cracked black pepper.

Cook in the oven for about 15 minutes, until the cheese starts to brown.

Remove from the oven then tuck in.

GARLIC PORTOBELLO PAPPARDELLE

Pasta sauces don't get much simpler than olive oil and garlic, and it's an all-time classic combination that goes so well with mushrooms. The trick with this dish is to first cook the mushrooms over a high heat to intensify the depth of flavour and extract all the water before adding the garlic (otherwise the garlic will burn). Using lasagne sheets, you can cut your own extra-wide pasta strips to create this elegant but simple Garlic Portobello Pappardelle.

To make 1 portion

1 portobello mushroom, sliced

3 dried lasagne sheets

2 garlic cloves, sliced

Pinch of dried (or chopped fresh) parsley

Grating of parmesan

Olive oil

Salt and pepper

To cook

Bring a pan of salted water to the boil.

Meanwhile, season and pan-fry the sliced mushroom in a big glug of olive oil over a medium-high heat for 8–10 minutes until dark brown in colour.

Cook the lasagne sheets in the boiling water until al dente, then drain and cut them into wide strips.

Add more olive oil to the mushroom, add the garlic and fry until the garlic just starts to colour. Now, add the pasta and fry for a further 30 seconds.

Remove from the heat and garnish with the parsley and a generous grating of parmesan.

CURRIED HALLOUMI & SPINACH

Pan-fried halloumi is such a treat. It takes on a gorgeous texture and the pan-frying process gives you the perfect opportunity to add bags of flavour to this versatile cheese. So, here, I have pan-fried it in Indian spices to create a delicious vegetarian curry that will pique the interest of any carnivore.

To make 1 portion

2 slices of halloumi cheese

1½ tsp korma curry powder

Handful of spinach

Splash of single cream

Olive oil

Salt and pepper

To cook

Pan-fry the halloumi slices in a splash of olive oil over a medium heat with 1 teaspoon of the korma curry powder and some cracked black pepper. Cook for a few minutes on each side and, once it starts to brown, remove from the pan.

Using the same pan, add some more olive oil if necessary, then add the spinach with the remaining curry powder and stir until it starts to wilt. Now, add the cream and stir for 30 seconds to create a creamy, curry-infused sauce. Taste and season, if required.

Serve the fried halloumi on a bed of the creamy curried spinach.

CHICKEN & MUSHROOM WITH TOBACCO FRIES

A while back, I became obsessed with cooking potatoes in all sorts of different and interesting ways, and these Tobacco Fries became a huge hit with my friends. They are like chips made from just the crunchy coating, with no soft middle bit – they add an amazing texture to this dish and are really moreish.

To make 1 portion

1 small floury potato, unpeeled

1 chicken thigh, de-boned

1 flat cap mushroom, sliced

1 tbsp crème fraîche

Olive oil

Salt and pepper

To cook

Preheat your oven to 190°C/gas mark 5.

Grate the potato with a cheese grater into a colander, rinse under cold running water to remove all the starch, then squeeze it with your hands to remove all the water. Spread out the grated potato on a non-stick baking tray, add a glug of olive oil and mix to coat evenly. Place in the oven for about 20 minutes, turning the fries every 5 minutes until they are evenly browned and crunchy.

Meanwhile, season the chicken thigh with salt and pepper and pan-fry it skin-side down in a splash of olive oil over a medium heat for 8 minutes until the skin is crispy. Turn the chicken over and cook for a further 8 minutes, until cooked through. Remove the chicken from the pan and set it aside.

Add the mushroom slices to the frying pan, adding more oil if needed, season and cook until they start to colour. At this point add the crème fraîche and a splash of water then stir to create a creamy mushroom sauce.

Serve the chicken thigh on a bed of the creamy mushrooms and top with the tobacco fries.

CUMIN-SPICED CHICKPEAS & SPINACH

This dish has a big Moroccan influence, and transforms these pretty normal ingredients into a hot and spicy treat. Adding an egg makes it a great brunch dish.

To make 1 portion

200g chickpeas (from a 400g tin), drained

1 tsp ground cumin

1 tsp hot paprika

Handful of spinach

1 egg

Olive oil

Salt and pepper

To cook

Put the chickpeas, a glug of oil, cumin, paprika and a pinch of salt and pepper in a frying pan over a medium heat and cook for a few minutes, then add the spinach. Continue to cook for a further minute then, once the spinach has wilted, transfer to a plate while you fry the egg.

Serve the fried egg with the spiced chickpeas, and some cracked black pepper, and finish by drizzling over some of the cumin and paprika-infused olive oil from the pan.

BEETROOT CARPACCIO

Get creative with your presentation skills and try this stunning Beetroot Carpaccio. The flavours are fresh and summery, making it ideal for a sophisticated al fresco lunch with a chilled glass of white wine and some bread.

To make 1 portion

1 pre-cooked beetroot, thinly sliced

Small handful of crumbled feta cheese

1 tsp crème fraîche

½ lemon

Olive oil

Salt and pepper

To prepare

Lay the thinly sliced beetroot on a plate in a circular formation so the edges overlap, then sprinkle over the feta.

To make the dressing, mix the crème fraîche with a big squeeze of lemon juice in a bowl then drizzle it over the beetroot.

Garnish with a few gratings of lemon zest, a splash of olive oil, a tiny pinch of salt and some cracked black pepper.

BAKED EGGS & ASPARAGUS

There are so many things you can do with eggs for brunch. These baked eggs have a lovely runny yolk to dip your asparagus into, then, at the bottom when the dipping fun is over, there are little chunks of feta cheese and some spinach to keep you interested and digging in until the very end.

To make 1 portion

Small handful of crumbled feta cheese

A few spinach leaves

2 eggs

A few asparagus spears

Olive oil

Salt and pepper

To cook

Preheat your oven to 190°C/gas mark 5.

Sprinkle the crumbled feta into an ovenproof ramekin or jar and add the spinach. Crack in the eggs and season with a pinch of salt and cracked black pepper.

Cook in the oven for about 15 minutes, until the egg white is cooked but the yolk is still a bit runny.

Meanwhile, coat the asparagus spears in a little olive oil and sprinkle with a small pinch of salt and pepper, then griddle (or pan-fry) until tender.

Serve your baked eggs with asparagus spears to dip.

BACON & ASPARAGUS TAGLIATELLE

A lot of pasta sauces follow similar formats, but this asparagus and bacon pasta dish uses the asparagus stalks creatively to make the sauce, giving it a powerful asparagus flavour, balanced with lovely smoky and salty bacon.

To make 1 portion

A few asparagus spears

A few rashers of smoked streaky bacon, roughly chopped

Handful of dried tagliatelle

Olive oil

Salt and pepper

To cook

Bring a pan of salted water to the boil.

Cut the top 4cm off each asparagus spear, set the tops to one side, and finely dice the rest. Pan-fry the diced asparagus and bacon in a splash of olive oil over a medium heat with a pinch of salt and pepper for about 5 minutes, until the asparagus has softened. Roughly mash the asparagus in the pan with the back of a fork, add the asparagus tips and continue to fry for a few more minut until the bacon is nicely coloured, adding a spla more olive oil.

Meanwhile, cook the tagliatelle in the salted boiling water until al dente.

Add the cooked tagliatelle straight from the boiling water into the pan with the asparagus and bacon using tongs, adding a splash of the starchy pasta cooking water to create the sauce.

Give it a little stir, and serve.

use panchetta time (ham).
soften your diced
asparagus first in
small pan of bo
water simmer til
add to your fr
panchetta then
asparagus tips.
its all cooking (
put on Pasta m

ASPARAGUS LASAGNE WRAP

This is my fast and fresh take on a classic lasagne using asparagus and mozzarella. All the key flavours are still there but the whole dish is lighter, more vibrant and takes a fraction of the time to prepare. So, as soon as asparagus season hits, grab some bargain spears and add this to the list of asparagus dishes you know how to cook.

To make 1 portion

1 dried (or fresh) lasagne sheet

A few asparagus spears

200g chopped tomatoes (from a 400g tin)

½ tsp dried oregano

¼ mozzarella ball

Olive oil

Salt and pepper

To cook

Preheat your oven to 190°C/gas mark 5.

Cook the lasagne sheet in a pan of salted boiling water until al dente (skip this step if you are using a fresh lasagne sheet).

Wrap the asparagus spears in the lasagne sheet and place in an ovenproof dish. Pour the chopped tomatoes around the wrapped asparagus, add the oregano, season with salt and pepper and add a glug of olive oil. Tear the mozzarella into chunks and lay them on top of the lasagne sheet.

Cook in the oven for about 20 minutes until the cheese has melted, the sauce has thickened and the asparagus spears are cooked.

SINGAPORE CHOW MEIN

Singapore Chow Mein is a great example of a fast, fresh and convenient meal in a bowl. It is also ideal for using up leftovers, so if you have some chicken left over from your Sunday roast or some random veg, then chuck them in too. The key to creating a really authentic looking home-cooked version is to use delicate vermicelli noodles.

To make 1 portion

¼ red onion, sliced

Sesame oil

¼ green pepper, sliced

1 spring onion, roughly chopped

1 garlic clove, sliced

Pinch of dried chilli flakes

Small handful of cooked and peeled prawns

½ tsp ground turmeric

½ tsp curry powder

1 sheet of dried vermicelli noodles

1 small egg

Salt and pepper

To cook

Bring a pan of salted water to the boil.

Fry the onion in a splash of sesame oil in a wok over a medium-high heat. After 30 seconds, add the sliced pepper, then after a further 30 seconds, add the spring onion, garlic and chilli flakes. Just before the garlic starts to brown, add a splash more sesame oil, the prawns, turmeric and curry powder.

Blanch the vermicelli noodles briefly in the boiling water, according to the packet instructions, then, as soon as they become soft, add them to the wok using tongs.

Scoop everything to one side of the pan and crack the egg into the empty side of the wok, allow it to start cooking, then, when it is about 75 per cent cooked, scramble it using a wooden spoon and mix it in with the noodles.

Season to taste with salt and pepper and serve.

ROAST CHICKPEA SALAD

Chickpeas are such a versatile storecupboard ingredient. They're great for bulking out meals, but they can also be used as the main ingredient. Here, I have oven-baked them in olive oil and spices to create a crispy coating that gives this salad an amazing texture.

To make 1 portion

200g chickpeas (from a 400g tin), drained

1 tsp ground cumin

1 tsp paprika

Small handful of rocket

Small handful of crumbled feta cheese

Olive oil

Salt and pepper

To cook

Preheat your oven to 190°C/gas mark 5.

Tip the chickpeas into an ovenproof dish along with the cumin, paprika and a generous glug of olive oil. Season with salt and pepper and bake for 30 minutes until golden brown.

Set the roasted chickpeas aside for a few minutes to cool down a bit.

To serve, mix the chickpeas with the rocket, crumbled feta and a glug of olive oil.

MUJADARRA WRAP

Traditionally a Middle Eastern rice dish topped with crispy fried onions, I wanted to use the flavours of mujadarra to create the ultimate wrap. So, I added some caramelised minced lamb to the onion topping and created a light and refreshing pea and mint sauce to give it all a lift.

To make 1 portion

½ mug of basmati rice

1 mug of water, plus 25ml for the flatbread

½ tsp ground turmeric

1½ tsp ground cumin

¼ red onion, sliced

100g minced lamb

40g plain flour, plus extra for dusting

1 tbsp crème fraîche

Small handful of frozen peas, defrosted

Pinch of dried mint

Olive oil

Salt and pepper

To cook

Put the rice and mug of water in a saucepan, add the turmeric and half a teaspoon of the cumin, bring to the boil and simmer gently, with the lid on, for about 10 minutes. When all the water has been absorbed and the rice is cooked, remove from the heat, uncover, and set aside until ready to serve.

While the rice is cooking, pan-fry the onion and minced lamb in a splash of olive oil along with the remaining cumin over a medium heat for about 10 minutes, until caramelised and golden brown.

To make the flatbread wrap, mix the flour and 25ml water in a bowl with a pinch of salt to form a dough. Dust the worktop with a little flour, then knead the dough on the worktop for a few minutes until smooth. Roll the dough out into a rough 20cm circle. Heat a dry frying pan over a high heat, add the flabread and cook for about 2 minutes on each side, until nicely toasted.

To make the sauce, mix the crème fraîche in a bowl with the defrosted peas and dried mint.

Assemble the wrap by scattering a layer of rice over the flatbread and topping it with the minced lamb and a big dollop of cool pea and mint sauce to finish.

LAMB MEATBALL TAGINE

This is a great example of how, with a few shortcuts, and by swapping lamb shoulder for lamb meatballs, you can transform a traditionally slow-cooked tagine into a super-quick and easy weekday supper.

To make 1 portion

100g minced lamb

2 garlic cloves, crushed

2 tsp ground cumin

¼ red onion, sliced

½ carrot, roughly sliced

200g chickpeas (from a 400g tin), drained

200g passata

½ mug of couscous

½ chicken stock cube

½ mug of boiling water

Olive oil

Salt and pepper

To cook

Combine the minced lamb in a bowl with half the crushed garlic, half the cumin and season with salt and pepper. Form the mixture into three or four meatballs and pan-fry them in a splash of olive oil over a medium heat for about 7 minutes until they start to brown. Add the onion and carrot to the pan and fry for a further few minutes. Just as the onion starts to brown, add the chickpeas, passata, remaining garlic and cumin and season with salt and pepper. Simmer for about 10 minutes until the sauce is reduced and the meatballs are cooked through.

While the meatballs are simmering, tip the couscous into a heatproof bowl, crumble in the stock cube, add the boiling water, stir and leave to stand for 7 minutes.

When everything is ready, fluff up the couscous with a fork and serve it with the lamb meatball tagine.

FISH EN PAPILLOTE

This is what frozen fish was made for: hassle-free and delicious meals at a moment's notice. Here, I have used an old technique of cooking ingredients in greaseproof paper – it locks in the moisture and steams the fish, potatoes and fennel. So, everything happens inside the parcel, leaving you with more free time and no washing up.

To make 1 portion

A few small potatoes, thinly sliced

½ fennel bulb, thinly sliced

1 frozen white fish fillet

Wedge of lemon (optional)

Olive oil

Salt and pepper

To cook

Preheat your oven to 190°C/gas mark 5.

Grab a square sheet of greaseproof paper and lay some sliced potatoes in the middle, season with salt and pepper, then add a layer of sliced fennel and place the frozen fish fillet on top. Add a glug of olive oil and season with a pinch of salt and plenty of cracked black pepper.

Wrap the paper around the fish and fold it tightly to make a parcel, then place it in the oven on a baking tray for about 40 minutes, until the fish is cooked through.

Unwrap the parcel and enjoy your meal straight from the paper, with a wedge of lemon if you like.

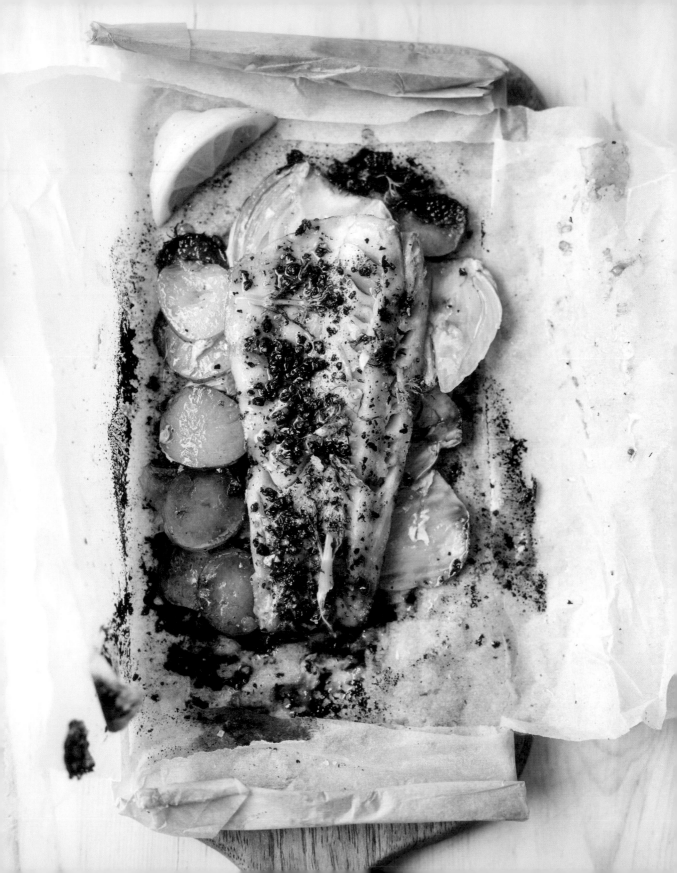

FALAFEL BURGER

Here's a fun take on a veggie burger, using a homemade pitta bun wrapped around my super-simple pan-fried falafel. I always try to do something extra special for my veggie followers on Instagram and I hope I've done them proud!

To make 1 portion

100g chickpeas (from a 400g tin), drained

½ carrot

1 spring onion

1 tsp ground cumin

½ tsp dried (or chopped fresh) parsley

1 egg, beaten

70g plain flour, plus extra for dusting

28ml cold water

A few slices of tomato

A few lettuce leaves

A few slices of red onion

Olive oil

Salt and pepper

To cook

Put the chickpeas, carrot, spring onion, cumin and parsley in a food processor or blender and pulse just a few times to make a rough paste. Tip the mixture out into a bowl, season well with salt and pepper, then stir in half the beaten egg and 2 teaspoons (about 10g) of the flour to give the falafel mixture a firm mashed potato consistency (adding a little more flour if necessary).

Split the mixture into two and form into patties. Pan-fry the patties in a splash of olive oil over a medium heat for 10 minutes, turning after about 5 minutes, until golden brown on both sides.

While the falafel patties are cooking, make the pitta 'bun'. Mix the remaining 60g flour, cold water and a pinch of salt in a bowl to form a dough. Dust the worktop with a little flour, then knead the dough on the worktop for a few minutes until smooth. Roll it out into a 15 x 5cm oval shape. Heat a dry frying pan over a high heat, add the pitta and cook for about 2 minutes on each side, until nicely toasted.

Assemble your burger by folding the pitta around the two patties and placing tomato slices, lettuce leaves and red onion between each layer.

CHICKEN WITH BLACK BEAN SAUCE

This One Pound Meals twist on a Chinese takeaway dish (one of my favourites) creates a great all-in-one meal. The black beans are the base carb and the addition of green beans transforms it into a well-balanced, nutritious version of a classic dish.

To make 1 portion

1 chicken thigh, de-boned

Sesame oil

1 garlic clove, sliced

Pinch of dried chilli flakes

200g black beans (from a 400g tin)

Soy sauce

Handful of green beans

Salt and pepper

To cook

Bring a pan of salted water to the boil.

Season the chicken thigh with salt and pepper and pan-fry it skin-side down in a splash of sesame oil over a medium heat for about 8 minutes, until the skin is crispy. Turn the chicken over and cook for a further 8 minutes, until cooked through. Remove the chicken from the pan and set it aside.

In the same pan you cooked the chicken in, add a splash more sesame oil (if required) and pan-fry the garlic and chilli flakes. After a minute, just before the garlic starts to colour, add the black beans (including half the liquid from the tin) and a splash of soy sauce and simmer for 5 minutes.

While the black beans are simmering, cook the green beans in the pan of boiling water.

After a few minutes, when the green beans are cooked (but still firm), plate up the black beans, then drain the green beans and add them to the dish, and top with the chicken thigh.

CAULIFLOWER & ROASTED TOMATO TABBOULEH

Oven-roasting cherry tomatoes magnifies their flavour and creates the most amazingly intense and tangy ingredient for this hot tabbouleh (I like to roast the tomatoes for as long as possible to intensify the flavour even more). Traditionally, tabbouleh is made with bulgar wheat and served cold as a salad or side dish to accompany grilled meats, but here, I have substituted the wheat for cauliflower and transformed it into a standalone vegetarian main dish.

To make 1 portion

A few cherry tomatoes, halved

1 red onion, quartered

¼ cauliflower

1 garlic clove, crushed

Pinch of dried (or chopped fresh) parsley

Olive oil

Salt and pepper

To cook

Preheat your oven to 190°C/gas mark 5.

Put the tomatoes and onion in an ovenproof dish, toss with a generous glug of olive oil, season with plenty of salt and pepper and roast for at least 30 minutes, until they start to colour.

Meanwhile, chop the cauliflower very finely, season it with salt and pepper and pan-fry it in a splash of olive oil over a medium heat. After about 10 minutes, as the cauliflower starts to soften, add the crushed garlic and continue to fry for a further 10 minutes until the cauliflower is cooked through but still has a bit of bite.

To serve, mix everything together while the tomatoes, onion and cauliflower are still warm, sprinkle with the parsley and dress with a little splash of olive oil and a pinch of salt and pepper.

BACON & KALE MINESTRONE SOUP

This is far more than just a soup. It is a super-speedy, warming and hearty main meal packed with vitamins and minerals. What I also love about this soup is that its chunky pieces of bacon and al dente pasta mean you are not compromising on texture and substance.

To make 1 portion

¼ white onion, sliced

3 rashers of smoked streaky bacon, roughly chopped

100g chopped tomatoes (from a 400g tin)

200ml water

½ beef stock cube

Small handful of macaroni

Handful of kale, chopped

Olive oil

Salt and pepper

To cook

Fry the onion and bacon in a saucepan in a splash of olive oil over a medium heat for a few minutes, until they start to brown. Add the chopped tomatoes and water, crumble in the stock cube and simmer for a few more minutes until slightly reduced, then add the macaroni and continue to simmer until the pasta is al dente, adding a little more water if required.

One minute before serving, add the kale and simmer until nicely wilted.

Add plenty of cracked black pepper, taste and add salt if required, and serve.

5-SPICE BAKED FETA & ASPARAGUS SALAD

Feta takes on a whole different texture when oven-baked and allowed to cool. Here, I have lightly dusted the feta in Chinese 5-spice before baking it, and paired it with raw asparagus ribbons to create a really unusual yet delicious Asian-inspired salad.

To make 1 portion

A few cubes of feta cheese

1 tsp Chinese 5-spice

A few asparagus spears

1 tsp sesame oil

1 tsp soy sauce

To cook

Preheat your oven to 190°C/gas mark 5.

Dust the feta cubes with the Chinese 5-spice, then place them on a non-stick baking tray and cook in the oven for about 15 minutes until they start to turn golden brown. Remove from the oven and allow to cool.

Next, using a potato peeler, slice the asparagus into ribbons and dress them with the sesame oil and soy sauce.

Arrange the dressed asparagus in a bowl and top with the 5-spice baked feta.

THAI SWEET BUTTERNUT CURRY

This sweet veggie curry has a little spicy kick to it. Butternut squash, sugar snap peas, honey and milk give the curry a lovely sweetness that acts as a refreshing balance to the hot chilli in the background.

To make 1 portion

½ mug of basmati rice

1 mug of water

2 slices of peeled butternut squash, cubed

¼ onion, sliced

2 garlic cloves, sliced

Pinch of dried chilli flakes

1 tsp ground turmeric

1 tsp plain flour

200ml milk

Handful of sugar snap peas

2 tbsp honey

Olive oil

Salt and pepper

To cook

Put the rice and water in a saucepan, bring to the boil and simmer gently, with the lid on, for about 10 minutes. When all the water has been absorbed and the rice is cooked, remove from the heat, uncover, and leave to cool.

While the rice is cooking, pan-fry the cubed butternut squash with the sliced onion for about 7 minutes in a splash of olive oil over a medium heat and add a pinch of salt and pepper. Just before the onion starts to colour, add the garlic and the chilli flakes. Fry for a further minute, then add the turmeric and flour. Fry for a minute, then gradually add the milk and simmer over a medium heat for about 15 minutes, stirring occasionally, until the squash is cooked through (add a splash more milk if it gets too thick).

Add the sugar snap peas along with the honey, season to taste with salt and pepper, then simmer for a minute or so until the peas are cooked.

Serve the curry in a bowl along with the rice.

SAUSAGE, KALE & BLACK BEAN STEW

By using tinned black beans as a clever cheat, this quick-cook stew has a rich depth of flavour normally associated with a much longer three- or four-hour cooking time. So, next time you're craving some comfort food, give this recipe a go.

To make 1 portion

2 sausages, cut into bite-sized chunks

1 garlic clove, sliced

200g black beans (from a 400g tin)

Handful of kale, chopped

Olive oil

Salt and pepper

To cook

Pan-fry the sausages in a splash of olive oil over a medium heat for about 15 minutes, until they are nicely coloured and cooked through, then add the garlic and fry for a further minute. Add the black beans (including half the liquid from the tin), season with salt and pepper and simmer for a few minutes before adding the kale (add a splash more water if you need to).

Simmer for a minute or so until the kale is nicely wilted, then serve with a generous pinch of cracked black pepper to garnish.

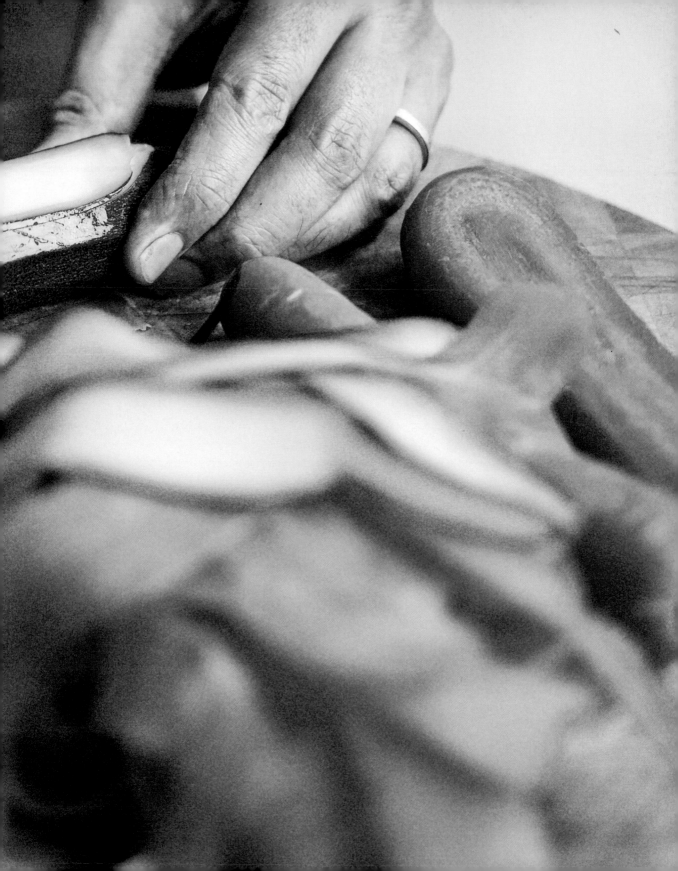

SPIRAL VEGETABLE TART

Looking at this dish, you might think you'd need fancy knife skills to pull it off, but the whole thing is a huge cheat! It's all done with a vegetable peeler. So, if you're looking for something impressive to post on Instagram or wow your friends and family with, then this is the dish for you. It involves very few ingredients, is easy to prep and has maximum visual impact.

To make 1 portion

½ red onion

1 courgette

1 carrot

1 potato

1 tsp dried oregano

1 egg

Olive oil

Salt and pepper

To cook

Preheat your oven to 190°C/gas mark 5.

Cut the red onion into very thin slices and then, using a vegetable peeler, cut the courgette, carrot and potato into thin strips. Lightly drizzle all the slices with olive oil, and season with some of the oregano and some salt and pepper.

Grab a few slices of each vegetable (don't forget the onion) and roll them into a small spiral on the worktop. Keep placing more strips of vegetables and slices of onion around the outside and build the spiral until it is roughly the size of your dish.

Crack the egg into the dish and whisk it with a fork, season with a pinch of oregano, salt and pepper, then place the spiral into the dish. Push the spiral down so the egg fills the small gaps in the spiral, then bake in the oven for about 30 minutes until the vegetables are cooked.

ROASTED ALOO GOBI

Roasted veg is the best, not least because you can cook it all in one tray! Here, I've just infused the veg with some lovely curry flavours to make one of my favourite One Pound Meals. Roasted Aloo Gobi is a great example of how oven-baking can freshen up a typically greasy dish.

To make 1 portion

¼ cauliflower, cut into small florets

1 potato, cubed

2 tsp curry powder

Handful of frozen peas

Handful of spinach

Olive oil

Salt and pepper

To cook

Preheat your oven to 190°C/gas mark 5.

Throw the cauliflower florets into an ovenproof dish along with the cubed potato. Drizzle with olive oil and sprinkle over the curry powder. Mix everything together and roast in the oven for 40 minutes.

After the vegetables have been roasting for 40 minutes, add the frozen peas, stir them in and roast for a further 5 minutes or until they are cooked. Remove the dish from the oven and stir in the spinach, using the heat of the roasted veg to wilt it.

Season with salt and pepper, then serve in a bowl.

MACKEREL FISH CAKES & PARSLEY SAUCE

This is a great recipe for a hot summer's evening. You'll love dipping the smoky, crispy fish cakes into the light, refreshing lemon and parsley sauce.

To make 1 portion

1 smoked mackerel fillet, flaked

2 tbsp breadcrumbs (grated stale bread)

1 spring onion, finely chopped

1 egg, beaten

2 tsp plain flour

125ml milk

1 tsp dried (or chopped fresh) parsley

Squeeze of lemon juice

Olive oil

Salt and pepper

To cook

Mix the flaked mackerel, breadcrumbs, spring onion, egg and 1 teaspoon of the flour together in a bowl to form the fish cake mixture. Season well with salt and pepper.

Heat a splash of olive oil in a pan over a medium heat and spoon the fishcake mixture into the pan in three dollops. Turn the fish cakes over after about 5 minutes, then fry for a further 5 minutes, until the middle is cooked through and the outside is golden brown.

Meanwhile, to make the sauce, add a tiny splash of olive oil to a pan over a medium heat and add the rest of the flour. Stir with a whisk and slowly add the milk to create a creamy sauce. When the sauce has thickened, season with salt and pepper and add the parsley and lemon juice.

Place the fish cakes in the middle of the lemon and parsley sauce.

PEA & FETA QUESADILLA

My Pea and Feta Quesadilla is a fantastic fresh and light alternative to a traditional quesadilla. A great idea for a quick lunch, it is jam-packed with vitamins from the peas.

To make 1 portion

Big handful of frozen peas

40g plain flour, plus extra for dusting

25ml cold water

50g feta cheese, crumbled

Salt and pepper

To cook

Defrost the peas in a colander under the hot tap for 1–2 minutes.

To make the tortilla, mix the flour and water in a bowl with a pinch of salt to form a dough. Dust the worktop with a little flour, then knead the dough on the worktop for a few minutes until smooth. Divide the dough into two balls and roll each piece into a roughly 10cm circle.

Heat a dry frying pan over a high heat, add the tortillas and cook for 20 seconds on each side (just long enough for them to hold their shape).

To make your quesadilla, lightly crush the peas in a bowl with the back of a spoon, then mix them with the crumbled feta and a pinch of salt and pepper. Sandwich the filling between the two tortillas.

Heat a dry frying pan or griddle pan over a high heat. Add the quesadilla and cook for about 5 minutes on each side, until the outside is nicely toasted.

CHILLI BEEF RAMEN

Making ramen is an excellent way of using up random leftover ingredients: almost anything can go in a ramen. Here, I have topped the whole thing off with lovely sticky chilli beef and a perfectly cooked egg with that all-important runny yolk.

To make 1 portion

1 egg

Small handful of minced beef

Sesame oil

1 garlic clove, sliced

Pinch of dried chilli flakes

1 tbsp honey

Soy sauce

1 spring onion, roughly chopped

150ml water

½ beef stock cube

1 sheet of dried rice noodles

¼ carrot, cut into strips

1 mushroom, sliced

Salt and pepper

To cook

Bring a pan of water to the boil and cook the egg for exactly 7½ minutes, then plunge it into cold water to stop the egg from cooking further.

Pan-fry the beef in a glug of sesame oil over a medium heat with a pinch of salt and pepper. After about 5 minutes, add the garlic and chilli flakes then continue to fry for a couple of minutes until the beef is golden brown. Add the honey and a splash of soy sauce then fry for a couple of minutes until the beef is lovely and sticky. Remove the beef from the pan and set it aside.

Throw the spring onion into the same pan you cooked the beef in, and after 1 minute, add the water and crumble in the stock cube. As soon as the water starts to bubble, add the rice noodles and simmer according to the packet instructions until cooked (add more water if you need to).

Peel the egg, then assemble the ramen. Lay the noodles at the bottom of the bowl, and place the spring onion, raw carrot, raw mushroom and chilli beef on top. Halve the egg and add it to the bowl, cut-side up. Ladle over the stock and finish with a drizzle of sesame oil, some cracked black pepper and a splash of soy sauce.

CHICKEN & TENDERSTEM STIR-FRY

I'm a big fan of the simple, core Chinese ingredients of garlic, chilli, sesame oil and soy sauce. With these flavours, you can take your favourite British-grown ingredients and transform them into exotic meals in minutes.

To make 1 portion

Handful of Tenderstem broccoli

1 chicken thigh, de-boned

Sesame oil

1 garlic clove, sliced

Pinch of dried chilli flakes

Soy sauce

Sprinkle of flaked almonds

Salt and pepper

To cook

Bring a pan of salted water to the boil and blanch the broccoli by cooking it briefly, just for a minute or two.

Meanwhile, season the chicken thigh with salt and pepper and pan-fry it skin-side down in a splash of sesame oil over a medium heat for about 8 minutes until the skin is crispy. Turn the chicken over and cook for a further 8 minutes, until cooked through.

Cut the chicken into strips and return it to the pan along with the garlic, chilli, a splash more sesame oil and the blanched broccoli. Fry for a few minutes, adding a splash of soy sauce towards the end. Serve in a bowl with a few flaked almonds and some cracked black pepper to garnish.

TARTE BIANCO

Potatoes, cream and onion are a classic French combination, but here I've replaced heavy and rich cream with tangy crème fraîche, and balanced it all on top of a super-simple and delicious homemade tart!

To make 1 portion

Sheet of puff pastry

2 tbsp crème fraîche

A few very thin slices of onion

A few small potatoes, very thinly sliced

Olive oil

Salt and pepper

To cook

Preheat your oven to 190°C/gas mark 5.

Using a round template, such as a cereal bowl, cut out a neat circle of puff pastry. Spread the crème fraîche over the top, scatter over the thinly sliced onion and season with salt and pepper.

Lay the thin slices of potato on top of the tart in concentric circles, slightly overlapping each slice. Drizzle with olive oil, season once more, then cook in the oven for about 40 minutes, or until the potatoes are golden brown.

£1 STICKY WINGS

This is one of my all-time favourite One Pound Meals. Chicken wings are so economical and take on flavours better than any other cut of meat. Here, I have quickly coated them in a super-speedy Chinese marinade, and because I cook them on top of the sweet potato, this all slowly soaks into the potato too!

To make 1 portion

1 tbsp sesame oil

1 tbsp soy sauce

1 tbsp honey

Pinch of dried chilli flakes

1 tsp Chinese 5-spice

1 garlic clove, crushed

4 chicken wings

1 sweet potato, peeled and cubed

1 spring onion, sliced

Salt and pepper

To cook

Preheat your oven to 190°C/gas mark 5.

Combine the sesame oil, soy sauce, honey, chilli flakes, Chinese 5-spice and crushed garlic in a bowl with a generous pinch of salt and pepper, add the chicken wings and coat them in the marinade.

Lay the sweet potato cubes in an ovenproof dish, throw the chicken wings on top and cook for about 45 minutes, or until the skin of the chicken wings turns a lovely golden brown and they are cooked through.

Set the wings aside and mash the sweet potato with the back of a fork, season with salt and pepper, then arrange the wings back on top and garnish with the spring onion.

CAPRESE CLUB

I can't think of many 'summer' sandwiches, so I took my favourite summer salad, a cool and refreshing Caprese salad, and modified the ingredients to create a club sandwich. Instead of butter, I have used creamy smashed avocado, and also brushed what would be a traditional olive oil dressing lightly on the bread with a pinch of oregano before toasting.

To make 1 portion

3 slices of bread

Pinch of dried oregano

½ ripe avocado

2 tomatoes, sliced

½ mozzarella ball

Olive oil

Salt and pepper

To cook

Lightly brush the bread slices on both sides with olive oil and scatter with the oregano before toasting on a hot griddle pan or frying pan.

Meanwhile, mash the avocado in a bowl with a pinch of salt and pepper using the back of a fork.

Once toasted, spread the smashed avocado on two of the bread slices, top with the sliced tomatoes and hand-torn chunks of mozzarella. Stack into a club sandwich and top with the final bread slice.

SPROUT & APPLE SALAD WITH GRILLED GOATS' CHEESE

This salad is so tangy and refreshing! The sprouts and apple complement the grilled goats' cheese, making for a perfectly balanced dish. I know a raw sprout and Granny Smith salad may sound a bit strange, but just give it a try and impress a few friends with your new avant-garde cooking skills.

To make 1 portion

1 slice of goats' cheese

A few sprouts

¼ Granny Smith apple

Juice of ½ lemon

Olive oil

Salt and pepper

To cook

Place the goats' cheese on a baking tray and cook under a hot grill for about 10 minutes, until the top is bubbling and starting to brown. Remove from the grill and allow the cheese to cool a bit.

Meanwhile, finely slice the sprouts and cut the piece of apple into very small matchsticks. Toss them together in a bowl with the lemon juice, a drizzle of olive oil and a pinch of salt and pepper.

To serve, arrange the sprout and apple salad in a bowl and top with the grilled goats' cheese.

SARDINE PASTA

Tinned sardines have all the flavour of the sea, and are ideal for a quick hassle-free pasta sauce. Chuck in a few salty olives and the whole dish comes together in minutes to create this Mediterranean classic.

To make 1 portion

125g dried spaghetti

¼ red onion, roughly diced

1 garlic clove, sliced

200g chopped tomatoes (from a 400g tin)

120g tin of whole sardines in oil, drained

A few black pitted olives

Olive oil

Salt and pepper

To cook

Bring a pan of salted water to the boil and cook the spaghetti until al dente.

Meanwhile, pan-fry the onion in a splash of olive oil over a medium heat for a few minutes. Add the garlic and, just before it starts to brown, add the chopped tomatoes and season well with salt and pepper. Next, add the sardines and black olives then simmer for 5 minutes to reduce the sauce.

Serve the sauce on a bed of the spaghetti, drizzle with a generous glug of olive oil and add an extra sprinkling of cracked black pepper.

PARTY PIZZAS

These quick and easy baked filo pizzas are fun finger food and great for packed lunches, parties or tasty snacks. They are so much more interesting than boring sandwiches wrapped in cling film.

To make 1 portion

6 square sheets of filo pastry (about 20 x 20cm)

Handful of cherry tomatoes, quartered

Handful of grated mature cheddar cheese

6 slices of chorizo

Pepper

To cook

Preheat your oven to 190°C/gas mark 5.

Grab a muffin tin and fold each sheet of filo in half, then in half again, to make six 10cm squares. Using your fingertips, press a filo square into six of the holes in the tin to create cup shapes. Throw in enough chopped cherry tomatoes to fill each cup about three-quarters full, season with pepper and top with some grated cheese and a slice of chorizo.

Cook in the oven for about 20 minutes, taking them out of the muffin tin after 10 minutes, placing them on a baking tray and putting them back in the oven for the final 10 minutes of baking. This guarantees the bases get nice and evenly toasted.

GRIDDLED VEGETABLE RAGU

This meat-free dish resembles a classic pasta ragu, with griddled aubergine giving texture to the sauce and the griddled courgette acting as the 'pasta' base. Vegetables take on a lovely smoky flavour when you griddle them and give this ragu a whole new dimension.

To make 1 portion

¼ aubergine, cut into 1cm-thick slices

1 courgette, cut lengthways into 2mm-thick slices

¼ red onion, roughly diced

1 garlic clove, sliced

200g chopped tomatoes (from a 400g tin)

Olive oil

Salt and pepper

To cook

Toss the aubergine and courgette slices in a bowl with a splash of olive oil and a pinch of salt.

Preheat a dry griddle pan over a high heat, then add the aubergine and cook in the griddle pan until soft and charred on both sides.

Meanwhile, pan-fry the onion in a splash of olive oil over a medium heat until soft but not coloured. Roughly dice the griddled aubergine and add it to the pan, and as soon as the onion starts to colour, add the garlic. Cook for a further minute, then add the chopped tomatoes. Simmer for a few minutes to thicken the sauce and season well with salt and pepper.

While the sauce is simmering, griddle the courgette slices. Once the slices are charred on both sides, arrange them on a plate and top them with the aubergine ragu.

CHERRY TOMATO & CHEDDAR SQUARE

This tart, with its base of mature cheddar cheese and topping of oven-roasted tomatoes, packs a powerful punch. It tastes a bit like pizza but has twice the intensity of flavour. If you are making it for a packed lunch or picnic, then a great idea is to cut the pastry base to exactly the size of your lunchbox, so it fits snugly.

To make 1 portion

15 x 15cm sheet of puff pastry

A few slices of red onion

Small handful of grated mature cheddar cheese

8 cherry tomatoes, halved

Pinch of dried oregano

Olive oil

Salt and pepper

To cook

Preheat your oven to 190°C/gas mark 5.

Lightly score a 1cm border around the puff pastry sheet with a knife and prick the inside square a few times with a fork (to stop it rising in the oven).

Lay the red onion slices on the puff pastry within the border, then sprinkle over the cheese. Toss the tomatoes in a little olive oil and a pinch of salt and pepper then position them evenly over the tart, cut side up. Finish with a sprinkle of oregano and cook in the oven for about 25 minutes, until the cheese is bubbling and the pastry is golden brown.

ASPARAGUS & GOATS' CHEESE DANISH

We've all seen the classic Danish pastry shape made with sweet fillings for breakfast and desserts. Here, I have transformed it into a savoury dish with an asparagus and goats' cheese filling, elevating the Danish pastry into a more sophisticated dish for vegetarians.

To make 1 portion

4 asparagus spears

10 x 10cm sheet of puff pastry

3 slices of goats' cheese

Milk, for brushing

Olive oil

Salt and pepper

To cook

Preheat your oven to 190°C/gas mark 5 and line a baking tray with greaseproof paper.

Toss the asparagus spears in a little olive oil and a pinch of salt and pepper, then lay them diagonally across the puff pastry sheet. Place the goats' cheese slices across the asparagus and gently wrap the filling in the pastry by folding the two side flaps over each other. Brush the pastry with a little milk, place on the lined baking tray and bake in the oven for 20 minutes until the pastry is golden brown.

BROAD BEAN SUMMER CASSOULET

This is my fast and fresh take on a French cassoulet. Instead of slow-cooking pork and white beans to create a heavy casserole, my summer update on this classic dish uses smoked bacon and broad beans in an uplifting, tasty vegetable broth with a hint of smokiness.

To make 1 portion

2 rashers of smoked streaky bacon, roughly chopped

½ carrot, roughly chopped

2 spring onions, roughly chopped

1 tsp plain flour

½ vegetable stock cube

200ml water

Small handful of frozen broad beans

2 slices of bread

Pinch of dried (or chopped fresh) parsley (optional)

Olive oil

Salt and pepper

To cook

Pan-fry the bacon and carrot in a splash of olive oil over a medium heat. Once the bacon is cooked and starting to colour, throw in the spring onions and the flour and cook, stirring, for a further minute, then crumble in the stock cube and add the water. Stir to dissolve the stock cube and simmer for a few minutes, then add the frozen broad beans. Season with salt and pepper and continue to simmer for a few more minutes until the carrots are cooked but still firm.

Serve the cassoulet with toasted bread drizzled in a little olive oil and salt, with a pinch of parsley to garnish, if you like.

BUTTERNUT GNOCCHI WITH CRISPY PARMA HAM & FETA

This is my fresh and colourful take on gnocchi, using squash instead of potato, and serving it as a bright and vivid summer salad with crispy pan-fried Parma ham, peppery rocket and flecks of bright white, tangy feta cheese.

To make 1 portion

250g cubed squash

1 egg yolk

1 tbsp plain flour, plus extra for dusting

2 slices of Parma ham, torn into pieces

Small handful of rocket

20g feta cheese, crumbled

Olive oil

Salt and pepper

To cook

Preheat your oven to 190°C/gas mark 5.

Coat the cubed squash in a splash of olive oil and season well with salt and pepper. Transfer to an ovenproof dish and bake for about 25 minutes, until soft.

Bring a pan of salted water to the boil.

Mash the roasted squash in a bowl with the back of a fork and season again. Stir in the egg yolk and flour to create a light dough that is not too sticky to shape (you can add more flour if needed). Dust the worktop with a little flour then very gently knead the gnocchi dough on the worktop for a minute until smooth.

Roll the dough into a long sausage shape, then cut it into 2.5cm sections and cook the pieces in the boiling water for about 5 minutes. Drain.

Pan-fry the gnocchi in a splash of olive oil over a medium heat, adding the Parma ham after a minute. Continue to fry for a few more minutes until the gnocchi starts to colour and the Parma ham gets nice and crispy.

Remove from the heat and serve on a bed of rocket, garnished with the crumbled feta and some cracked black pepper.

SUMMER CHICKEN PIE

This is a summer version of my classic pub-style chicken pie from my first book. To freshen it up, I have substituted the puff pastry with a crunchy filo top and made a light and lemony chicken filling.

To make 1 portion

1 chicken thigh, de-boned, skin removed and diced

2 spring onions, chopped

1 tsp plain flour

125ml milk, plus extra for brushing (optional)

¼ lemon

Sheet of filo pastry

Olive oil

Salt and pepper

To cook

Preheat your oven to 190°C/gas mark 5.

Season the chicken with salt and pepper, then pan-fry it in a splash of olive oil over a medium heat for about 10 minutes, until the chicken starts to brown. Add the spring onions and stir in the flour, then fry for a further minute. Gradually add the milk, stirring continuously, to create a creamy sauce. Taste and season once more, then squeeze in the juice from the lemon quarter.

Transfer the chicken filling to a small ovenproof dish and top with a scrunched-up sheet of filo. For a lovely golden brown top, you can also brush the filo with a tiny splash of milk.

Cook the pie in the oven for about 20 minutes, or until the filo is a lovely golden brown colour.

PORK STIR-FRY WITH SUGAR SNAP PEAS

This is a really simple stir-fry using thinly cut strips of pork that cook in no time at all. The honey in the sauce give a lovely sticky and glossy finish to the dish and helps the flavour to cling to the pork and the crunchy sugar snap peas.

To make 1 portion

½ mug of brown rice

1 mug of water

1 pork loin chop, cut into thin strips

Sesame oil

1 garlic clove, sliced

Pinch of dried chilli flakes

Small handful of sugar snap peas

2 tbsp honey

Soy sauce

Salt and pepper

To cook

Put the rice and water in a saucepan and bring to the boil. Simmer gently, with the lid on, over a low heat until all the water is absorbed and the rice is cooked.

Meanwhile, season the pork with salt and pepper and pan-fry it in a splash of sesame oil over a medium heat for about 5 minutes, until the meat starts to brown. Add the garlic, chilli flakes, sugar snap peas and a splash more sesame oil. Fry for a further couple of minutes, then add the honey and a generous splash of soy sauce. Stir constantly for 2 minutes as the sauce thickens and coats everything, then, before it burns, remove the pan from the heat.

Serve the pork and sugar snap peas with the rice.

SPEEDY CHORIZO BOLOGNESE

Pan-fried chorizo goes so well with a tangy tomato passata. As the sauce bubbles away, the tomato flavours intensify and mix with the spicy paprika-infused oil from the chorizo to create a totally different style of bolognese. And, thanks to all these strong flavours, this lovely rich and intense sauce can be made in just minutes.

To make 1 portion

Handful of dried tagliatelle pasta

A few slices of cooking chorizo

2 spring onions, roughly sliced

200g passata

Olive oil

Salt and pepper

To cook

Bring a pan of salted water to the boil and cook the tagliatelle until al dente.

Meanwhile, pan-fry the chorizo slices in a glug of olive oil over a medium heat for a few minutes until they start to colour. Add the spring onions and continue to fry for a further minute before adding the passata. Season well with salt and pepper, add another glug of olive oil and simmer for a few more minutes until the sauce is reduced.

Serve the sauce with the pasta and sprinkle with cracked black pepper.

SMOKY FISH TACOS

Using smoked mackerel gives these fish tacos an extra smoky flavour with zero extra effort! Just throw the ingredients in the pan (the mackerel is already cooked so making the filling takes just minutes), then simply knock up a few tortillas and it's summer time.

To make 1 portion

¼ red onion, roughly diced

200g chopped tomatoes (from a 400g tin)

1 smoked mackerel fillet, flaked

1 tsp ground cumin

1 tsp paprika

40g plain flour, plus extra for dusting

25ml cold water

3 tsp crème fraîche

1 spring onion, sliced

1 lemon wedge, to serve (optional)

Olive oil

Salt and pepper

To cook

Pan-fry the onion in a splash of olive oil over a medium heat then, as soon as the onion starts to soften, throw in the chopped tomatoes, flaked mackerel, cumin and paprika. Season well with salt and pepper and simmer for about 10 minutes to reduce the sauce.

Meanwhile, combine the flour, water and a pinch of salt in a bowl to form a dough. Dust the worktop with a little flour, then knead the dough on the worktop for a few minutes until smooth. Divide the dough into three balls and roll each piece into a roughly 10cm circle. Heat a dry frying pan over a high heat, add the flatbreads and cook for about 2 minutes on each side until lightly toasted.

Now, assemble the tacos (while the flatbreads are still warm). Spoon a little of the mackerel and tomato mixture onto each taco, add a teaspoon of crème fraîche on top and garnish with the sliced spring onion to add a bit of extra crunch. Serve with a lemon wedge, if you like.

PORK SALTIMBOCCA & GREEN PEA MASH

The Parma ham gives an extra salty and slightly smoky dimension to the pork in this dish, and goes well with the hint of sweetness from the pea mash. There's nothing unusual about the ingredients used here, but by cooking them in a fun and interesting way, you'll be more motivated to cook at home.

To make 1 portion

1 large potato, peeled and roughly cubed

Handful of frozen peas

1 pork loin chop, halved

1 slice of Parma ham, halved

Olive oil

Salt and pepper

To cook

Cook the cubed potato in a pan of salted boiling water until soft, then add the peas and bring back to the boil. As soon as the water reaches the boil, drain, then return the potato and peas to the pan and mash them with a splash of olive oil and plenty of salt and pepper.

Meanwhile, season the pork pieces with salt and pepper, wrap them in the Parma ham and pan-fry in a splash of olive oil over a medium heat for about 6 minutes on each side (the cooking time will depend on the thickness of the pork chop). Once cooked through, remove from the heat and create a quick jus by deglazing the pan with a splash of water.

Lastly, pile the mash on a plate, balance the pork saltimbocca on top and drizzle over the jus.

PORK CHAR SUI

This is another fun example of what can be achieved with pretty straightforward ingredients and a bit of imagination. It's definitely not how you're supposed to make char sui, but it's a cheeky £1 version you can cook at home to put a smile on your face.

To make 1 portion

1 tsp paprika

1 tsp Chinese 5-spice

2 tsp soy sauce, plus extra to serve

2 tsp sesame oil

1 pork loin chop

2 tsp honey

A few spring onions, halved

Salt and pepper

To cook

Combine the paprika, Chinese 5-spice, soy sauce and sesame oil in a bowl with a pinch of salt and pepper. Coat the pork loin chop in the mixture.

Pan-fry the pork over a medium heat for about 7 minutes on each side, taking care not to burn the coating too much. When the pork is almost cooked through, add the honey to the pan and baste the pork with it for a few minutes, to create a sticky glaze. Remove the pork from the pan when it's cooked through and set it aside.

Fry the spring onions in the pan with the leftover glaze for a minute or two.

Cut the pork char sui into pieces at an angle and serve it with the glazed spring onions and a splash of soy sauce.

CAJUN CHICKEN WITH CREAMED CORN

Creamed corn is a big favourite of mine, but all the preparation and simmering it requires makes it a bit too complicated for just one portion. So, the simplest way to enjoy it at home is to treat it almost like a sweet potato mash. I just grab a tin of corn, blend it, season it, and heat it up in a small saucepan.

To make 1 portion

1 tsp Cajun spice blend

1 chicken thigh, de-boned

½ red pepper, halved

198g tin of sweetcorn

Olive oil

Salt and pepper

To cook

Combine the Cajun spice and a pinch of salt and pepper in a bowl with a glug of olive oil and coat the chicken thigh in the mixture. Pan-fry the chicken slowly over a low–medium heat (to ensure the Cajun spice doesn't burn) for about 15 minutes on each side, until cooked through. When cooked, remove the chicken from the pan and set it aside.

Pan-fry the red pepper in the same pan for a few minutes on each side, until soft and lightly charred.

Meanwhile, roughly blitz the sweetcorn (with the liquid from the tin) in a blender or food processor with a big pinch of salt and pepper. Transfer to a saucepan and simmer for a few minutes to thicken.

Serve the chicken on a bed of the creamed corn and pan-fried pepper.

HALLOUMI KEBAB

I love the way that the Parma ham crisps up around these halloumi cubes – together, they create one of the tastiest mouthfuls of kebab you'll ever eat. By cooking the couscous in the same pan as the kebab, it takes on the kebab's flavours and you get a mellower version of the same savoury notes.

To make 1 portion

1 slice of Parma ham, quartered

100g halloumi, cut into 4 cubes

1 spring onion, sliced

¼ mug of couscous

¼ mug of water

Olive oil

Salt and pepper

To cook

Wrap each piece of Parma ham around a cube of halloumi, pushing the wrapped cubes onto a skewer if you wish (you don't have to use a skewer).

Pan-fry the wrapped halloumi cubes (skewered or as they are) in a splash of olive oil over a medium heat for 8 minutes, turning them every couple of minutes until each side is golden brown. Remove from the pan and set them aside.

Fry the spring onion in the same pan with a splash more olive oil for a few minutes until soft, turn the heat off and add the couscous to the pan, followed by the water. Stir, season lightly with salt and pepper, and leave to stand for 5 minutes.

To serve, fluff up the couscous with a fork and serve it with the halloumi cubes laid on top.

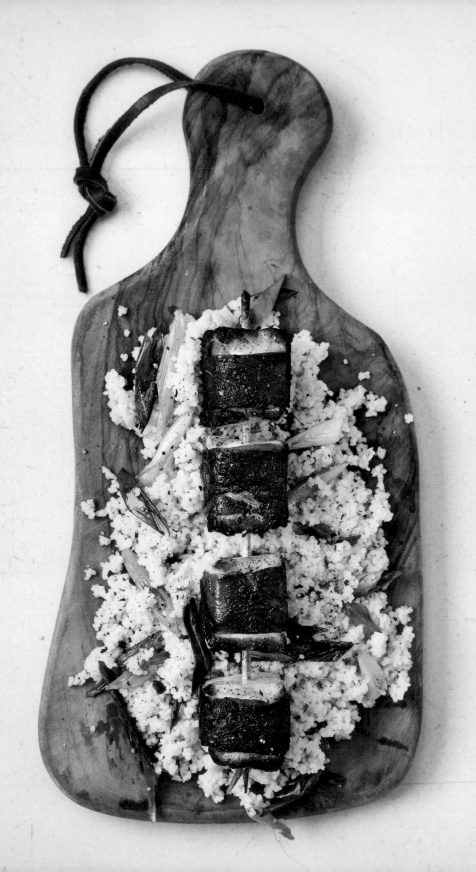

NEPTUNE PIZZETTI

I really love the flavours of a traditional Neapolitan marinara pizza, especially as the garlic, drizzled with olive oil and sprinkled with a pinch of salt, sizzles away in the heat, infusing its flavours into the sauce. Here, I have created the ultimate crispy pizzetti base, then taken it one step further, adding smoked mackerel to create these delicious extra-crunchy Neptune Pizzetti.

To make 1 portion

40g plain flour, plus extra for dusting (if needed)

25ml cold water

3 tbsp passata

1 garlic clove, sliced

A few black olives

½ smoked mackerel fillet, flaked

Olive oil

Salt and pepper

To cook

Preheat your oven to 190°C/gas mark 5 and line a baking tray with greaseproof paper.

Mix the flour and water with a pinch of salt in a bowl to form a dough. Tip the dough onto the worktop and knead it for a few minutes until smooth (dusting the worktop with flour if it is too sticky). Roll the dough out into three evenly sized oval shapes about 2mm thick then place them on the lined baking tray.

Spread 1 tablespoon of passata onto each pizzetti, adding the sliced garlic, olives and flakes of smoked mackerel. Sprinkle with salt and pepper, finishing with a drizzle of olive oil.

Bake for about 20 minutes, until the bases are crisp and the garlic is sizzling (but not burnt!).

For a nice rustic effect, serve the pizzetti on the greaseproof paper.

BAKED GOATS' CHEESE FRITTATA

The secret ingredient in this baked frittata, which makes it so soft and gooey, is a tablespoon of crème fraîche. Also, the frittata takes on an amazing flavour as the goats' cheese melts and combines with the cracked black pepper and kale.

To make 1 portion

2 eggs, beaten

1 tbsp crème fraîche

Handful of kale

A few slices of goats' cheese

Salt and pepper

To cook

Preheat your oven to 190°C/gas mark 5.

Combine the eggs in a bowl with the crème fraîche and kale. Season with salt and pepper and pour the mixture into an ovenproof dish. Top with slices of goats' cheese and bake for about 20 minutes, until the top of the frittata starts to turn a lovely golden brown.

HOT SALAD NIÇOISE

Here I have updated one of the most famous salads of all time to create a warm smoked version with a zingy mustard dressing and a gooey soft-boiled egg. This recipe uses just one saucepan of boiling water to cook the three hot elements of the dish, saving you time and washing up.

To make 1 portion

1 egg

Handful of green beans

A few cherry vine tomatoes (on the vine)

1 tsp Dijon mustard

1 smoked mackerel fillet, flaked

A couple of slices of red onion

Olive oil

Salt and pepper

To cook

Bring a pan of salted water to the boil, add the egg and cook for 7½ minutes. Once boiled, use a spoon to take the egg out of the water then stop the egg cooking any further by cooling it under cold running water. Add the green beans and tomatoes to the boiling water and remove after a few minutes, once the beans are cooked and tender and the tomatoes have softened.

Meanwhile, mix the Dijon mustard with 2 teaspoons of olive oil to create a dressing.

Peel the boiled egg, cut it in half and serve it with the beans, tomatoes, flaked smoked mackerel and onion. Finish the dish with a drizzle of the Dijon dressing and a pinch of salt and pepper.

PEA & PEARL BARLEY RISOTTO

Dry grains make great storecupboard ingredients as they last for ages and can bulk out a meal at a moment's notice. Here, I've made a quick barley risotto with just a handful of frozen peas (another essential I always have to hand!) and some leftover feta.

To make 1 portion

¼ onion, roughly diced

Handful of pearl barley

½ vegetable stock cube

Handful of frozen peas

10g feta cheese, crumbled

Olive oil

Salt and pepper

To cook

Pan-fry the onion in a splash of olive oil over a medium heat and add a pinch of salt and pepper. Once it starts to soften, add the pearl barley, crumble in the stock cube and add 100ml of water.

As the risotto simmers and the pearl barley absorbs the water, keep adding more water, little by little, continuing to stir. Once the pearl barley is soft and cooked (after 15–20 minutes), taste and season again if required, then stir in the peas. Once the peas are cooked, serve the risotto with the crumbled feta on top.

STUFFED LEEKS

These stuffed leeks have a salty, cheesy, soft filling and a gorgeous garlicky, crunchy topping. This dish is ideal comfort food, helps you to use up that leftover feta and gives you another reason not to throw away that stale bread.

To make 1 portion

1 leek

Handful of crumbled feta cheese

Handful of breadcrumbs (grated stale bread)

1 garlic clove, crushed

Olive oil

Salt and pepper

To cook

Preheat your oven to 190°C/gas mark 5.

Cut the leek in half lengthways, then cut each half into two sections about 7.5cm long. Remove the inner layers to create a cavity and fill the cavities with the crumbled feta.

To make the breadcrumb topping, mix together the breadcrumbs, crushed garlic and a glug of olive oil in a bowl and season with salt and pepper.

Lay the stuffed leeks in a small ovenproof dish and sprinkle over the breadcrumb mix. Cook in the oven for about 20 minutes, until the breadcrumbs are golden brown.

PAD THAI

I had my work cut out using everyday ingredients to simplify this complex dish. But I managed to replicate the flavour of sweet palm sugar and salty fish sauce with my new secret ingredient: peanut butter!

To make I portion

1 sheet dried flat rice noodles

Sesame oil

1 garlic clove, sliced

Pinch of dried chilli flakes

¼ red onion, sliced

A few slices of carrot, cut into matchsticks

1 spring onion, roughly chopped

Small handful of cooked and peeled prawns

1 tbsp crunchy peanut butter

1 egg

Soy sauce

To cook

Pre-cook or soak the rice noodles, according to the packet instructions.

Heat a glug of sesame oil in a pan or wok over a high heat. Add the garlic, chilli flakes and red onion and stir-fry for 30 seconds, then add the carrot and spring onion. Stir-fry for a further minute, then add the prawns and peanut butter. Continue to cook for a minute or so until everything is cooked.

Scoop everything to one side of the pan and crack the egg into the empty side. When the egg is 75 per cent cooked, scramble it using a wooden spoon and mix it in with the rest of the ingredients, also adding the drained noodles. Finish with a generous glug of soy sauce and serve immediately.

FISHERMAN'S PIE

Frozen fish is the key to the simplicity of this dish. You can just chop it and throw it in straight from the freezer and this easy-to-follow recipe takes care of everything else to create a beautiful creamy sauce with a vibrant pea mash and crunchy topping.

To make 1 portion

1 potato, peeled and roughly cubed

Handful of frozen peas

½ onion, chopped

1 tsp plain flour

200ml milk

1 frozen white fish fillet

Small handful of breadcrumbs (grated stale bread)

1 garlic clove, crushed

Olive oil

Salt and pepper

To cook

Preheat your oven to 190°C/gas mark 5.

Cook the potato in a pan of salted boiling water until soft, then add the peas and bring back to the boil. Drain, then return to the pan and mash the potato and peas with a splash of olive oil and season with salt and pepper.

Meanwhile, pan-fry the onion in a splash of olive oil over a medium heat for a few minutes until soft but not browned, season well with salt and pepper and add the flour. Stir for a minute, then slowly add the milk, stirring continuously, to create a sauce.

Cut the frozen fish fillet into bite-sized chunks using a serrated knife and add them to the sauce. Simmer for 5 minutes to defrost the fish, then transfer the mixture to a small ovenproof dish. Spoon the mash over the fish filling.

Combine the breadcrumbs, a splash of olive oil, a pinch of salt and pepper and the crushed garlic in a bowl then scatter them over the pie to create the crunchy topping.

Cook the pie in the oven for about 20 minutes, until it is golden brown on top and the filling is piping hot.

ULTIMATE £1 ROSTI

My Ultimate £1 Rosti stack is the perfect weekend brunch treat: a crispy nest of potato topped with a layer of fresh spinach, baked Parma ham and a luxurious poached egg to finish.

To make 1 portion

1 small potato, grated

¼ onion, finely sliced

1 slice of Parma ham

1 egg

A few spinach leaves

Olive oil

Salt and pepper

To cook

Preheat your oven to 190°C/gas mark 5.

Rinse the grated potato in a sieve under cold running water to wash off the starch, then squeeze out the excess water and mix it in a bowl with a splash of olive oil, a pinch of salt and pepper and the sliced onion. Shape into a patty (by hand or using an egg ring) and cook in the oven on a baking tray for about 20 minutes, until golden brown. About halfway through, scrunch up the Parma ham (to roughly the diameter of the rosti) and throw it onto the baking tray.

Meanwhile, bring a pan of water to the boil and poach an egg by cracking it into a mug, very slowly lowering it into the water, then very gently tipping it out. After a few minutes, once it's cooked, remove the egg with a slotted spoon.

Assemble the rosti stack by placing a few spinach leaves on the rosti, then the baked Parma ham and topping it all with the poached egg and cracked black pepper.

CHICKEN & MUSHROOM ORZO

I love using this simple one-pan style of cooking to create rustic-looking dishes: it is exactly the sort of food I like to eat at home and it's way less complicated than it looks.

To make 1 portion

1 chicken thigh, de-boned

A few mushrooms, sliced

A few spring onions, roughly chopped

1 garlic clove, sliced

Handful of orzo pasta

50ml water

Olive oil

Salt and pepper

To cook

Season the chicken thigh generously with salt and pepper and pan-fry it skin-side down in a splash of olive oil over a medium heat for 8–10 minutes until the skin is extra crispy. Turn the chicken over and cook for a few more minutes, then add the mushrooms, spring onions, garlic and a pinch of salt and pepper. Let everything fry together until the mushrooms are cooked and the garlic starts to colour, then add the orzo and water.

Stir to deglaze the pan and let everything simmer for 15–20 minutes (adding more water if needed). Once the water is absorbed and the chicken and orzo are cooked, season to taste and serve.

CAULIFLOWER STEAK

By basting cauliflower in butter, look how this boring vegetable has been transformed into an amazing steak. The creamy beans act as a sauce and really set the dish off.

To make 1 portion

Thick slice of cauliflower

1 tbsp butter

1 garlic clove, sliced

100g haricot beans (from a 400g tin), drained

100ml single cream

Small handful of spinach

Olive oil

Salt and pepper

To cook

Season the slice of cauliflower generously with salt and pepper and pan-fry it in a splash of olive oil with the butter over a medium heat for 15–20 minutes, turning it over every 3–4 minutes while continuously basting it with the melted butter using a tablespoon. When the cauliflower is a lovely golden brown colour, remove it from the pan and set it aside.

Meanwhile, in a separate pan, fry the garlic in a splash of olive oil over a medium heat, and just before the garlic starts to brown, add the haricot beans, then the cream. Season with a pinch of salt and pepper and, as the sauce starts to simmer, add the spinach and allow to wilt.

Serve the creamy haricot beans and spinach with the cauliflower steak.

BUTTERNUT PHO

By pan-frying big slices of butternut squash with the seeds still attached, the seeds get lovely and toasted, giving this dish a totally unexpected extra dimension of flavour and texture.

To make 1 portion

1 slice of butternut squash with seeds still attached, halved

Sesame oil

1 garlic clove, sliced

Pinch of dried chilli flakes

1 spring onion, roughly chopped

200ml water

½ vegetable (or beef) stock cube

Soy sauce

1 sheet of dried flat rice noodles

Salt and pepper

To cook

Season the butternut squash with salt and pepper and pan-fry it in a splash of sesame oil over a medium heat for 10 minutes, making sure the seeds get toasted too. Once the squash starts to brown and caramelise, add the garlic, chilli flakes, spring onion and a splash more sesame oil. Fry for a few minutes until the garlic starts to brown, then pick out some of the seeds to use as a garnish later.

Pour the water into the pan, crumble in the stock cube and add a splash of soy sauce. Simmer for 10–15 minutes, adding more water if necessary, until the squash is cooked through, then add the noodles and cook them in the broth for the time stated on the packet instructions.

Serve the butternut pho in a bowl with a splash more soy sauce and scatter with the toasted seeds and some cracked black pepper.

ROAST CARROTS, LENTILS & FETA DRESSING

We already know that oven-roasted carrots are amazing: they take on a whole new flavour as their sugars gently caramelise in the oven. But we're going to go one step further and transform them into something quite special, offsetting roasted carrot and lentils with an extremely simple, tangy feta dressing.

To make 1 portion

2 carrots, sliced lengthways

Handful of puy lentils

200ml water

½ vegetable (or chicken) stock cube

20g feta cheese, crumbled

Olive oil

Salt and pepper

To cook

Preheat your oven to 190°C/gas mark 5.

Throw the sliced carrots onto a baking tray, adding a glug of olive oil and a generous pinch of salt and pepper. Roast for about 30 minutes, until the edges of the carrots start to caramelise.

Meanwhile, add the lentils to a pan with the water and crumble in the stock cube. Simmer for about 20 minutes until all the water has been absorbed and the lentils are cooked.

To make the dressing, simply mix the feta in a bowl with a splash of water until all the lumps are gone.

To serve, season and plate the lentils, then top them with the roasted carrots and generously spoon over the feta dressing.

LAMB SAMOSAS

These are my quick and healthy no-fry curried Lamb Samosas (see pages 176–177 for my vegetarian version). By using filo pastry and oven-baking them, you get an amazing crunchy outside without the need for any oil.

To make 1 portion (5 samosas)

¼ red onion, diced

½ potato, cut into small cubes

½ carrot, cut into small cubes

Small handful of minced lamb

1 tsp curry powder

Small handful of frozen peas

A few sheets of filo pastry

Milk, for brushing

Olive oil

Salt and pepper

To cook

Preheat your oven to 190°C/gas mark 5.

Pan-fry the onion, potato and carrot in a splash of oil over a medium heat with some salt and pepper for a few minutes, then add the lamb mince and curry powder and cook for about 15 minutes.

Meanwhile, defrost the peas in a colander under the hot tap, and when the potato is soft and the lamb is nicely browned, stir them into the pan.

Cut a long rectangular piece of filo pastry and wrap the filling in the pastry (see following pages for step-by-step pictures). Repeat with the rest of the filling and more rectangular pieces of pastry. Brush the samosas with milk and bake in the oven on a non-stick baking tray for about 15 minutes until golden brown.

PEA & FETA SAMOSAS

With the samosa step-by-step on pages 174–175, you can now invent all sorts of cool fillings, and one of my favourites is a fresh and vibrant pea and feta filling, ideal for any lunchbox.

To make 1 portion (5 samosas)

Handful of frozen peas

30g feta cheese, crumbled

A few sheets of filo pastry

Milk, for brushing

To cook

Preheat your oven to 190°C/gas mark 5.

Defrost the peas in a colander under the hot tap, then mix in a bowl with the crumbled feta to create the filling.

Cut a long rectangular piece of filo pastry and wrap the filling in the pastry (see previous pages for step-by-step pictures). Repeat with the rest of the filling and more rectangular pieces of pastry. Brush the samosas with milk and bake in the oven on a non-stick baking tray for about 15 minutes until golden brown.

SWEETCORN, COURGETTE & FETA FRITTERS

By adding chunks of crumbled feta to these fritters, you get little pockets of intense flavour that make this dish so much more exciting to eat than your usual fritters. I like to top them with a poached egg and use the yolk as a kind of super-rich dipping sauce.

To make 1 portion

¼ courgette, cut into matchsticks

100g sweetcorn (from a 200g or 400g tin), drained

2 eggs

2 tbsp plain flour

20g feta cheese, crumbled

Small handful of rocket

Olive oil

Salt and pepper

To cook

Combine the courgette, sweetcorn, one of the eggs, the flour and crumbled feta in a bowl with plenty of salt and pepper.

Split the mixture into three and form into patties. Pan-fry the patties in a splash of oil over a medium heat for about 5 minutes on each side until golden brown and cooked through.

Meanwhile, bring a pan of water to the boil and poach an egg by cracking it into a mug, very slowly lowering it into the water, then very gently tipping it out. After a few minutes, once it's cooked, remove the egg with a slotted spoon.

Stack the fritters on a plate with some rocket and top with the poached egg and some cracked black pepper.

CHORIZO & RED PEPPER ORZOTTO

Orzo is a dream come true for making quick and super-simple recipes on a budget. Ready in minutes, you just throw it in the pan and watch it plump up as it absorbs all of the flavours in the dish. Here, in this speedy take on a risotto, it takes on the tomato passata and paprika-infused oil from the fried chorizo.

To make 1 portion

Handful of sliced cooking chorizo

½ red pepper, cut into wide slices

2 spring onions, roughly chopped

Small handful of orzo pasta

100g passata

Olive oil

Salt and pepper

To cook

Pan-fry the chorizo in a splash of olive oil over a medium heat. After a few minutes, as the chorizo starts to colour, add the red pepper slices and fry for a further couple of minutes, then add the spring onions. When the onions are soft, season well with salt and pepper, add the orzo, stir to combine and add the passata. Simmer for about 15 minutes, until the orzo is cooked, season with plenty of cracked black pepper, add more salt if needed, then serve.

SAUSAGE & KALE OMELETTE

This is how I like my omelettes to look: a bit like a sandwich, and always with something interesting and tasty poking out of the middle. The pan-fried sausage meat goes golden brown and crisps up beautifully to give this omelette an amazing texture.

To make 1 portion

1 sausage

Handful of kale

3 eggs

Olive oil

Salt and pepper

To cook

Cut a line down the length of the sausage, through the skin, and take out the meat.

Pan-fry the sausage meat in a splash of olive oil over a medium heat for 5–10 minutes, until it turns golden brown and crispy, then throw in the kale and continue cooking for a couple of minutes until it is wilted and cooked. Season with salt and pepper, remove from the heat and set aside.

Crack the eggs into a bowl and whisk them together. Heat a splash of oil in a separate frying pan, pour in the eggs and start to cook over a medium heat. When the omelette is 90 per cent cooked but still soft on top, add the omelette filling and gently fold the omelette over it. Continue to cook for a further minute, then serve.

CHURRASCO BURGER

This classic peri-peri-inspired chicken burger was a huge favourite at a high street fast-food chain until one day they took it off the menu. This news made headlines! So, I simply had to recreate it for everyone to enjoy once more.

To make 1 portion

2 tsp smoked paprika

1 chicken thigh, de-boned

1 spring onion, thinly sliced

1 small wedge of red cabbage, shredded

½ carrot, cut into matchsticks

2 tbsp crème fraîche

1 bun

Olive oil

Salt and pepper

To cook

Mix half the paprika in a bowl with a glug of olive oil and a pinch of salt and pepper. Add the chicken and coat it in the spiced oil, then fry it slowly, skin-side down, in a dry pan over a low–medium heat for 10–12 minutes, taking care not to burn the paprika. Turn it over and cook for a further 10–12 minutes, until the chicken is cooked through.

Meanwhile, make a coleslaw. Combine the sliced spring onion, shredded cabbage and carrot matchsticks in a bowl with half the crème fraîche and add a pinch of salt and pepper.

To make the piri piri mayo, mix the remaining crème fraîche with the rest of the paprika.

Assemble the burger by cutting the bun open, spreading the piri piri mayo on the bottom half, placing the chicken on top and finally adding the coleslaw before topping with the other half of the bun.

KEEMA RICE POT

This rice pot is packed with flavour, creating an exciting lunch you'll definitely look forward to more than a boring sandwich. Pre-cook the ingredients, pack them into a jar, then bring the whole thing alive with some boiling water.

To make 1 portion

¼ mug of basmati rice

½ mug of water

50g minced lamb

1½ tsp curry powder

A few spinach leaves

¼ beef stock cube

Olive oil

Salt and pepper

To cook

Put the rice and water in a saucepan, bring to the boil and simmer gently, with the lid on, for about 10 minutes. When all the water has been absorbed and the rice is cooked, remove from the heat, uncover, and leave to cool.

Meanwhile, pan-fry the lamb in a splash of olive oil over a medium heat with 1 teaspoon of the curry powder and a pinch of salt and pepper for 10–15 minutes until cooked and golden brown. Remove from the heat and leave to cool.

Grab a jar and lay the cooled rice at the bottom, then the spinach, then the cooled minced lamb. Crumble the stock cube over the lamb and sprinkle over the remaining curry powder.

Seal with a lid and store in the fridge (you can make it the night before you need it), then just add boiling water until it comes about three-quarters of the way up the jar, close the lid, give it a good shake and let it stand for 3 minutes before eating.

CHORIZO-STUFFED SWEET POTATO

This is my posh take on an American sports bar favourite. My fully loaded potato skins take less than ten minutes to prepare, and have a luxuriously rich and creamy filling with spicy chorizo but absolutely no melted cheese in sight.

To make 1 portion

1 sweet potato

Small handful of sliced cooking chorizo

2 spring onions, chopped

4 tsp crème fraîche

Olive oil

Salt and pepper

To cook

Pierce the sweet potato with a fork and cook it in a microwave for 7 minutes until the middle is soft and gooey (alternatively, bake it in the oven for about 30 minutes).

Meanwhile, pan-fry the chorizo in a splash of olive oil over a medium heat, adding the spring onions as soon as the chorizo starts to colour.

Cut the cooked sweet potato in half lengthways and scoop out the middle, adding it to the chorizo pan along with half the crème fraîche and plenty of salt and pepper. Stir everything together for a minute over a medium heat, then spoon the filling back into the sweet potato skins.

Serve with a dollop of crème fraîche on each half.

STICKY CHILLI BEEF BAO

Here, I have recreated one of my go-to Vietnamese street food dishes: a gorgeous sweet and fluffy steamed bun. I rarely made these at home because it was such a chore, but then I devised a huge shortcut by using self-raising flour instead of yeast. Now I make them all the time, with loads of different fillings – this sticky chilli beef version is one of my favourites.

To make 1 portion

40g self-raising flour, plus extra for dusting

20ml cold water

1 tsp honey, plus 1 tbsp for the beef

50g minced beef

Sesame oil

1 garlic clove, sliced

Pinch of dried chilli flakes

½ tsp Chinese 5-spice

Soy sauce

A few slices of carrot, cut into thin strips

A few slices of spring onion, cut into thin strips

Salt and pepper

To cook

To steam the bun, we first have to improvise a steamer. Grab a saucepan, fill it a quarter full of water, place a colander on top and find either a lid or a plate to sit on top of the colander (it is important that the water does not touch the base of the colander). Turn on the hob and bring the water to the boil.

To make the dough, grab a bowl, add the self-raising flour, water and teaspoon of honey, along with a pinch of salt and mix to form a dough. Dust the worktop with a little flour, then knead the dough on the worktop for a few minutes until smooth. Roll the dough out into a 10 x 5cm oval shape and fold it in half. Place on a square of greaseproof paper and pop it in the steamer, with the lid on, for about 10 minutes, until it is puffed up and fluffy.

Meanwhile, pan-fry the minced beef in a splash of sesame oil with a pinch of salt and pepper over a medium heat for about 10 minutes. Once it starts to brown, throw in the garlic, chilli flakes and Chinese 5-spice. Continue to fry for a few minutes, then add the remaining honey and a splash of soy sauce. Cook for a further 1–2 minutes until it is nice and sticky.

Cut the steamed bun along the fold and fill it with the sticky chilli beef and some carrot and spring onion strips to garnish.

CHICKEN NOODLE SOUP

This is a speedy way to feel good. A nice bowl of Chicken Noodle Soup is just what the doctor ordered! Here, I have added another One Pound Meals shortcut and cooked the noodles in the same pan as the chicken, as this adds flavour to the broth and also saves on washing up.

To make 1 portion

1 chicken thigh, de-boned

2 spring onions, halved

½ carrot

200ml water

1 chicken stock cube

1 sheet of dried egg noodles

Olive oil

Salt and pepper

To cook

Season the chicken thigh with salt and pepper and pan-fry it skin-side down in a splash of olive oil over a medium heat for 8 minutes, until the skin is crispy. Turn the chicken over and cook for a further 8 minutes, until cooked through. Remove the chicken from the pan and set it aside.

Add three of the spring onion halves to the same pan (saving the remaining half for garnish) and peel strips from the carrot using a vegetable peeler, adding them to the pan too. Fry for a couple of minutes to soften the vegetables then add the water and crumble in the stock cube. Bring to the boil and reduce the heat to a simmer, then add the noodles and cook according to the time stated on the packet instructions.

Once the noodles are cooked, transfer them to a bowl with the vegetables and some of the stock. Cut the fried chicken into pieces at an angle, and place them on top of the noodles. Chop the remaining spring onion half and sprinkle it over the bowl.

CHICHAROS

This is a Spanish dish that uses up leftover bread to create amazing croutons that suck up the paprika-infused oil from pan-fried chorizo. The chorizo and fried bread is then pepped up with vivid green peas to create a nicely balanced plate of food.

To make 1 portion

Small handful of sliced cooking chorizo

Small chunks of stale bread

1 egg

Handful of frozen peas

Olive oil

Salt and pepper

To cook

Pan-fry the chorizo in a splash of olive oil over a medium heat for a few minutes, then throw in the bread chunks and gently pan-fry them in the paprika-infused oil.

Fry the egg in a splash of oil in a separate pan.

Meanwhile, defrost the peas in a colander under the hot tap. Add them to the chorizo and croutons pan along with a pinch of salt and pepper. Cook for a minute or two until the peas are piping hot, then serve with the fried egg on top.

CHICKEN & CHICKPEA STEW

The quicker the stew, the fresher and more vibrant it is. So, this is my fast and fresh take on a classic Spanish chickpea stew, with all those smoky paprika flavours. Pan-frying the chicken separately brings the cooking time in at under 20 minutes, and also allows the dish to be presented in an elegant stack to show off each ingredient to its fullest.

To make 1 portion

1 chicken thigh, de-boned

¼ onion, sliced

1 garlic clove, sliced

200g chickpeas (from a 400g tin), drained

200g chopped tomatoes (from a 400g tin)

2 tsp smoked paprika

Small handful of spinach

Olive oil

Salt and pepper

To cook

Season the chicken thigh well with salt and pepper and pan-fry it skin-side down in a splash of olive oil over a medium heat for 8 minutes until the skin is crispy. Turn the chicken over and cook for a further 8 minutes, until cooked through.

Meanwhile, in a separate pan, fry the sliced onion over a medium heat in a splash of olive oil for 2 minutes, then add the garlic. Just before the garlic starts to brown, add the chickpeas and chopped tomatoes, season well with salt and pepper, then stir in the smoked paprika. Simmer for 10 minutes until the sauce is reduced.

Once the chicken is cooked through, spoon the chickpea stew into a shallow bowl, add a pile of spinach and top the spinach with the chicken thigh.

Finish with a little drizzle of olive oil and some cracked black pepper.

ROASTED CAULIFLOWER SALAD

Trust me on this, the best part of the cauliflower is actually the outer leaves. By drizzling them with some olive oil, seasoning them with salt and pepper, then baking them in the oven, you can create something amazing from an ingredient you would ordinarily just throw away. So give it a try and see what you think, I'm sure you'll be pleasantly surprised.

To make 1 portion

½ cauliflower (including outer leaves)

Olive oil

Salt and pepper

To cook

Preheat your oven to 190°C/gas mark 5.

Cut the cauliflower into medium florets, toss them into a roasting tray with a glug of olive oil and a generous seasoning of salt and pepper, then cook in the oven for about 20 minutes. Halfway through cooking, toss the cauliflower leaves in a glug of olive oil and season generously with more salt and pepper and add them to the roasting tray.

The cauliflower should be served as a warm salad, drizzled with the olive oil and seasoning from the roasting tin.

POT NOODLE

People are always asking me how they can make their packed lunches more exciting. Well, imagine tucking into a steaming hot jar of noodles with fresh crunchy veg and roast chicken tomorrow at work! This is a great way to use up leftover chicken after a Sunday roast. Just make your Pot Noodle on Sunday night, chuck it in the fridge and don't forget to take it to work on Monday morning.

To make 1 portion

1 chicken thigh or drumstick, or a few slices of leftover roast chicken

½ sheet of dried egg noodles

1 spring onion, roughly chopped

A few mangetout

1 mushroom, sliced

Pinch of dried chilli flakes

½ tsp paprika

½ tsp Chinese 5-spice

½ chicken stock cube, crumbled

Salt and pepper

To prepare

If you don't have any cooked chicken, roast the chicken thigh or drumstick in the oven for 30 minutes, until cooked through. Cut the cooked chicken into slices and lay them at the bottom of your jar. Put the egg noodles on top of the chicken, then add the remaining ingredients and season with a little salt and pepper.

Seal with a lid and store in the fridge until you're ready, then simply fill the jar with boiling water until everything is covered, close the lid, give it a little shake, wait for 3 minutes, then open the lid and slurp away.

PESCE AL FORNO

By oven-roasting a few simple ingredients with just olive oil and loads of pepper, you can create a wonderfully rich and intense sauce. As the tinned tomatoes and garlic slowly bubble away in this fish dish, their flavours magnify, while the fish slowly cooks on top. This is an easy, no mess, one-dish recipe that takes minutes to prep and throw in the oven.

To make 1 portion

200g chopped tomatoes (from a 400g tin)

1 garlic clove, crushed

A few black pitted olives

½ tsp dried oregano

1 frozen white fish fillet

Olive oil

Salt and pepper

To cook

Preheat your oven to 190°C/gas mark 5.

Grab a small ovenproof dish and tip in the chopped tomatoes, then add the garlic, olives and season with the oregano and some salt and pepper.

Place the frozen fish fillet on top and drizzle with a very generous glug of olive oil, sprinkling the fish with a pinch of salt and loads of cracked black pepper.

Cook in the oven for about 30 minutes, until the fish is cooked and starts to flake, then remove from the oven and serve.

INDEX

ISBN 9781472245632
eISBN 9781472245649

Commissioning Editor: Muna Reyal
Art Direction and Design: Superfantastic
Photography: Dan Jones
Project Editor: Kate Miles
Copy Editor: Laura Nickoll
Proofreader: Ilona Jasiewicz
Indexer: Caroline Wilding

Printed and bound in Germany by Mohn Media
Colour reproduction by Born London
Typeset in Brandon Grotesque, Avenir, Billabong

Headline's policy is to use papers that are natural, renewable and recyclable products and made from wood grown in sustainable forests. The logging and manufacturing processes are expected to conform to the environmental regulations of the country of origin.

HEADLINE PUBLISHING GROUP
An Hachette UK Company
Carmelite House
50 Victoria Embankment
London EC4Y 0DZ

www.headline.co.uk
www.hachette.co.uk